PRAISE FOR

THE FLOUNDERING FOUNDER

"If there is one book any budding B2B entrepreneur should read this year, it's this one. Raman brilliantly captures the realities of growing a small business in a smart and honest way while delivering lots of takeaway actions to improve your business and life. I read it in under three hours. A must-read!"

—Sara Davies, MBE, Dragon on BBC's *Dragons' Den*
and Founder of Crafter's Companion

"I wish only that Raman Sehgal had written this book forty years ago and made me read it. The Floundering Founder is filled with wisdom and advice that would have made my own journey happier and more productive. It can do that for you if you take its lessons to heart."

—Bo Burlingham, bestselling author
of *Small Giants* and *Finish Big*

"We need more people in this world who take responsibility for making themselves and people around them better. Raman is one of those people. He just gets shit done."

—Tucker Max, four-time
New York Times bestselling author

"Raman does a wonderful job of highlighting the importance of focusing your business on a niche while simultaneously dedicating yourself to personal development. A very enjoyable reading experience from beginning to end."

—Gino Wickman, author of
Traction and *Entrepreneurial Leap*

"Raman is a master of implementing what he has learned to drive amazing results. He shares specific steps you can follow to replicate his success. Each step is concise, actionable, and rooted in integrity. Most importantly, they are proven steps that you can follow, just as he has, to grow professionally and personally. Get on the same side with your goals."

—Ian Altman, bestselling author and
Forbes and *Inc.* columnist

"If you're ever looking for a coach, a mentor, or just a very entertaining traveling companion, Raman Sehgal is the winning ticket. Not only is his own career journey quite fascinating; he's also graced with the ability to draw sensible, down-to-earth lessons from that experience. You'll enjoy the chance to get to know him via the pages of this book. And by the time you're finished, you'll be surprised at how much more you know about your own strengths, challenges, and goals."

—George Anders, author of *The Rare Find* and *You Can Do Anything* and senior editor at large at LinkedIn

THE
FLOUNDERING
FOUNDER

24 LESSONS TO REFOCUS YOUR BUSINESS AND BETTER YOURSELF

RAMAN SEHGAL

LIONCREST
PUBLISHING

THE FLOUNDERING FOUNDER
24 Lessons to Refocus Your Business and Better Yourself

ISBN   978-1-5445-2722-2   *Hardcover*
       978-1-5445-2721-5   *Paperback*
       978-1-5445-2720-8   *Ebook*

Mum and Dad—I am forever grateful.

Selena and my boys, Niko, Enzo, and Ari—all in, forever.

Thank you x

CONTENTS

HOW TO MAKE A HORRIBLE FIRST IMPRESSION

by Fiona Cruickshank, OBE

You know they always say to make a good first impression?

Raman didn't.

He no-showed on his first day working for me, but I still ended up investing in his business over a cup of tea, getting married on the same day (not to each other), and making a lifelong friend.

Raman hasn't failed to delight and infuriate me in equal measure since that first day I thought he blew me off.

I was in my early thirties and a single mum living west of Newcastle, England. I'd built my business, The Specials Laboratory, from the ground up. Everything was going swimmingly. In nine years we expanded to five sites and employed almost 300 people, all with no external investment.

I'd taken on a marketing agency to help with PR; Raman was the fourth account executive assigned to my account. The churn at this place was outrageous.

I was busy and didn't have time for nonsense, so you can imagine my reaction when "number four" didn't show up to our first meeting.

Turns out Raman was not to blame. The agency had forgotten to let me know he was off sick. The irony? I think it's the only sick day he's taken in his entire life.

When twenty-two-year-old Raman finally bounced in the door (the man doesn't walk), I was such a cow to him.

Unphased, he won me over and did a fantastic job.

No mean feat.

I've backed him to the hilt ever since.

I'll be honest. I don't work anymore because I don't have to, or want to. I've established, grown, and exited several businesses over the last twenty-five years. Now I spend my time and money behind the scenes investing in other people's ideas and steering ships. I like it that way.

I am an introvert—a bullish one who knows how to get things done, mind you. But my ego doesn't need stroking, and I hate the spotlight.

Writing this foreword should be deeply unpleasant.

It's not.

Because I believe in Raman Sehgal, and I feel strongly that you should read *The Floundering Founder*.

By picking up this book you're signing up to learn from someone who has woven their generous, kind, whip-smart, and loveable personality through the fabric of an incredibly successful, mission-fuelled, people-first business.

Raman just can't help being himself. He's living proof that being a good person makes you a successful one.

In *The Floundering Founder*, Raman's written an honest, light-hearted, and deadly serious book about the many pot-holes that pave the road to starting, growing, and scaling a business. And he's broken it down into easy-to-read, bite-sized chunks, completely free of gobbledygook management speak.

Why try to impress people when being yourself takes care of business?

Whether you're just starting out, mid-flounder, or looking for some fresh ideas, this book will meet you where you're at, shed some light, and save you some skinned knees. It will get you somewhere quicker than you ever could on your own steam; something I always try to do with people I mentor.

Don't get me wrong. You're still going to make a mess once you read *The Floundering Founder*. That's part of it. Running a successful business means you need to have the balls to say, "I don't know. I messed up. But I'll figure it out."

I've seen Raman handle this better than anyone.

His unbridled enthusiasm for life and learning, and his pursuit of self-improvement is infectious.

Annoying sometimes too.

Back in the day I used to sponsor the British Pharmaceutical Students Association as my way of giving back. Raman was still handling my marketing at the time. We spent a couple of days tossing out freebies and drinking far too much in a godforsaken corner of Nottingham, UK.

One evening we'd gone out with our colleague, Elaine. We didn't even bother eating. We just drank and drank and drank.

The next morning was obscene.

The hotel had chosen our visit to commence construction work. Elaine and I were sitting in the foyer trying to nurse ourselves back to life. I thought I was going to be sick.

Suddenly, there was Raman. Bouncing down the stairs.

"You'll never guess what I've seen!"

He's brandishing a copy of the *New York Times* in my face. "Look, look, look!"

And, just like any *normal* twenty-two-year-old, he'd drawn a huge circle around a very specific article about the drugs industry that was so relevant to my business it was ridiculous.

I stared at the young man in front of me, grinning as enthusiastically as my head was pounding.

"What the hell is wrong with you, Raman!"

But that's Raman to a tee.

He's always on, even when he's not.

If Raman is Tigger, I am Owl. Eeyore, sometimes. We're an odd couple in business. We think about things very differently, but our values are tightly aligned. Which brings me back to investing in his company over a cup of tea.

Our days of doling out free pens together were long gone, but Raman and I were fast friends. I'd informally mentored him as his business, *ramarketing*, grew rapidly from bedroom-based startup to international agency.

One day Raman called me.

He was floundering.

"I haven't got a bloody clue what I'm doing. I'm in over my head. I need your help. Do you fancy investing so it's proper?"

We met up for tea, and in five minutes we'd decided how much money I was going to invest in ramarketing and what percentage I was going to get. The whole thing was as unusual as it was appropriate for the weird and wonderful working relationship we've built over the years. The lawyers and accountants involved thought we were bonkers, but within seventy-two hours, we'd signed an agreement, the money had gone in, and we were off and running.

Because it was never about the money with us.

Raman didn't need me to punt him a few thousand pounds. There was no hole to dig out of. We were simply formalising our relationship as shareholders and business partners. We were committing to doing good work together.

Business isn't always logical, but the right moves always make sense.

It would be lush if growing a business was as simple as a cup of tea. It's not, but you know that already or you wouldn't have picked up a book called *The Floundering Founder*.

Whether you're at the start of it all, in the messy middle, or feeling a little long in the tooth with your business, I'll wrap this up with the same advice I give Raman when he's in a tizzy.

Don't moan about taxes, even if it's the accountant's fault. Taxes are proof you're making money.

You're going to cock up. But Raman deposited $100,000 into the wrong company account and is still doing just fine. He'll tell you about that in the book.

Being open and funny and kind doesn't preclude you from being successful.

I don't care what the most embittered, blokey founder says, owning a business is emotional. And if you don't think it is, you haven't got the balls to be honest.

For the record, I'd take an honest person over a slick founder any day.

And lastly, take a page out of this book and just be yourself. If not bouncy like Raman, enthusiastic, curious, and hard-working in your own way.

With experience and responsibility comes efficiency and maturity, but the Raman I know hasn't changed at all.

He's grown. There's more of him. There's more about him.

He still has no business sending me a Calendly link rather than calling me immediately when I want to speak to him, but no one gets it right all the time.

Raman would be the first to admit that!

—Fi

IMAGINE.
AND SEE CLEARLY.

"Someone once told me the definition of hell; on
your last day on earth, the person you could have
become will meet the person you became."

—Anonymous

Take a breath. Think about that for a moment in the context of your life.

Just imagine if these people were miles apart. Gut-wrenching.

Chilling, right?

When I first heard this quote, it literally jolted my brain. What if the person I meet is so much better than who I became? I'd be devastated and full of regret.

As a founder, owner, or entrepreneur (however you like to categorise yourself) of a service business that was established based on your expertise, you have an ability to create something from nothing. I think it's fair for me to assume you can imagine, daydream, and let your mind wander. So, I have a fun exercise for you. Rather than thinking about your last day on earth (a bit morbid for the start of a book), let's simply fast forward your life by ten years.

Imagine yourself walking into your favourite bar or cafe. Picture every detail in your mind—the smell, the sounds, the noise, the ambience. It should bring a smile or sense of comfort to your soul.

In the corner of the venue is someone sitting at a table who looks very familiar. Strikingly similar, in fact. And kind of good-looking too. Because that person is you. Not you of today. It's you in ten years' time.

Naturally, you take a seat opposite your older self. Once you get past the initial shock and concern that this moment may in fact make the universe explode, you settle into a conversation. Your senior version offers some advice as to how you can make the most of the next decade. Put another way, what *they* wish they had done if they could have their time again.

Take a pen. Or open your digital notes. And write down exactly what you think they would say to you.

"I should have done...what?"

"I wish I had...what?"

If you dig deep and do this properly, it'll give you a list. Whether it's one thing, three, or nine. These are words of wisdom from your future self about what you *must* do in the next decade; otherwise, you'll regret it.

The goal of this exercise is to reengineer your long-term goals. Rather than focus on what you *think* you need to do, now you can focus on the things you'll regret if you don't make a plan today and start working towards your goals right away.

In Derek Sivers's most recent book, *How to Live*, he says, "We overestimate what we can do in one year. We underestimate what we can do in ten years." The sensational Mr. Sivers is absolutely right.

And make no mistake, the things you'll unlock by going through this exercise will be much farther reaching than "lose twenty pounds this year" or "save 10 percent of your paycheque every month." Those are hollow resolutions your future self won't be concerned with. Do this right and you will have a few powerful, thought-provoking, life-changing goals.

When I did this, my imagination unearthed what in my heart of hearts I knew I'd regret in the future if I didn't start moving on right away. The goals were sitting deep in my subconscious, and this exercise helped me unlock them and acknowledge their value.

I did this when I was thirty-five (six years after I started my company) and was going through what my wife describes as a mini, pre-midlife crisis. Truth is, I was floundering. Here are a few things that emerged from my subconscious:

- I wanted to have a third kid.
- I decided to say "fuck it" to doubt and see how far I could take my company.
- I had a deep desire to see more of the world in work and life.
- I recognised the importance of teaching my kids another language.

Having these goals rise to the surface and written down

almost lit the path ahead. I felt a sense of relief mixed with a large dose of excitement.

Now it's your turn. Stop and do this exercise before you continue with the rest of the book. You may need to repeat it a few times to get clear on what you really want to do and, most importantly, what you'll regret if you don't do. Based on the fact that you're holding this book right now, you also likely want to push your budding business as far as possible. The good news is you're in the right place.

This is not a book on how to start a business or scale up simply for the sake of growth. It's about intentionality, choice, and focus. Doing the things today that will benefit you for many years. It's also a book about you as a human being. If you improve your life, your business will improve too. If you stand still, your business will stall at best. You took the brave step to use your expertise to create a service-providing company. You're on an entrepreneurial journey, seeking to help others with your knowledge. Now it's time to stop floundering and focus on what truly matters.

MY JOURNEY

I was an ordinary kid like billions all over the world. An average C-grade student who graduated into a normal entry-level job. Loud, outgoing, and personable, yes. Beyond that, just like everyone else. But with spikey hair, a sizable nose, and a loud voice for a little fella.

In 2009, after a few years in different roles, I founded a marketing company called ramarketing. The name was one a friend and I imagined after a few drinks one night. We laughed at it, but it stuck. So, with just a single client and my tiny dining table, I got to work. It was a side-gig, done in my spare time alongside my day job as head of marketing for a pharmaceutical contract manufacturing organisation. It was created purely to earn some extra income that enabled my wife, Selena, and I to see more of the world in our early years of marriage. No fancy startup story. No fundraising. No aha moment. Simply an opportunity, which I'm glad I didn't pass.

Despite being spectacularly "ordinary" from an intellect perspective, I've since grown ramarketing, year-on-year, every year (30–70 percent on average). Today, it is a multi-million-dollar global digital marketing, creative, and content agency that focuses on life sciences with a presence in the US, Europe, and Asia. In 2021, it was named as the fastest growing communications agency in the UK by *PRWeek*. Nine years into growing the business, I relocated my family from the northeast of the UK to the northeast of the US to spearhead our North American business. We are proudly a genuine rarity for a service business headquartered in Northeast England.

I've also worked to become a published author, podcaster, international keynote speaker, blogger, guest university lecturer, and marathon runner. I've founded a few other niche businesses too. All have required courage, discipline, and focus—common themes you'll find in this book. I travel all over the world for work and have built a pretty decent international network. I'm also very happily married with three amazing kids, live in a nice house in Boston, and rarely work weekends.

At the time of writing this book (in 2021), people seem to see me as pretty successful—whatever that means. Some think this all happened overnight. And that could not be further from the truth. None of it happened by accident. Any successes I've enjoyed took serious work within my business and within myself. It's my genuine honour to share my mistakes and learnings with you in this book, to help you on your journey.

WHY I WROTE THIS BOOK

Take yourself back to the venue where you met your older self. Imagine walking out after this rather enchanting encounter with a list written down and a clearer idea of what's truly important to you. With that image in mind, let's revisit the opening quote.

> Someone once told me the definition of hell; on your last day on earth, the person you could have become will meet the person you became.

This book is a response to that quote—a guide to make sure that experience never happens. It's time to become more intentional and focused, my friend.

This book is about snapping out of autopilot, avoiding the drift, and overcoming that floundering feeling. Rather than shouldering those emotions of frustration, disorientation, and uncertainty on your own, you now have a guide. I didn't have a playbook; it was pure trial and error. And I've taken all that I have learnt from the last decade and neatly packaged it into twenty-four valuable insights for you and where you are right now. Put simply, this is what I did and what worked for me. If I was back in that space of floundering again, this is exactly what I'd do.

Even if you're a seasoned, battle-hardened business owner or service professional, my book will be a timely kick up the backside. A chance to reflect and maybe reset in the post-pandemic world we live in. A useful checklist of what not to overlook. Both in your business and yourself. A chance to kickstart some small, daily steps that turn into non-negotiable, essential habits. Enabling you to feel the reward from routine.

Don't get me wrong. No matter where you are and where you want to go, you have to put in the effort. Sacrifice, courage, and discipline are core components of the journey. That said, these twenty-four real-life, practical, doable lessons can help you find focus and direction. No ivy league education required, but no quick, shortcut hack to the top. You're taking the steep, spiral stairs of an ancient British castle rather than a modern elevator in a New York skyscraper.

Get yourself a coffee and a notebook. Let's do this.

Much love,
—Raman

PART
ONE

REFOCUS YOUR BUSINESS

One of the major downsides of writing a book is that I can't talk to you. More accurately, I do all the talking but don't get to listen to you and hear your thoughts. Since I can't know everything about you, I'm going to imagine a bit. I suspect you've already built up professional knowledge and developed skills in a particular area. Your interest in this book makes it safe to guess that you've used your expertise as the foundation of your own service-providing business, and you've created something from nothing. Whether you're in year two or twenty, you've accomplished something truly amazing.

In my mind, you've already accomplished one of life's most difficult challenges. You have taken your craft and turned that into a revenue-generating company. Whether your expertise is in marketing, PR, sales, accounting, design, or business consulting, it doesn't matter. It's all incredible. You are a founder.

Over the last decade, I've had the fortune of meeting many amazing people just like you. Courageous, ambitious folks who have taken a risk and created something from nothing. A living, breathing entity from scratch. The type of thing billions dream of, but you have *actually* done. Don't underestimate this tremendous achievement. Bravo!

If you're anything like these remarkable people, you may feel a little lost or stuck in a rut. It happens to almost all of us at some point. We hit a wall that makes us feel almost incapable. Maybe you are feeling guilty and frustrated with yourself because you just can't seem to find the time to escape the shackles of the day-to-day to work on improving your business and yourself. Maybe you're asking, "What now? Where next?„ It's a crossroad where each step forward doesn't feel exactly right. Your confidence and belief are weakening. It feels like you're floundering.

If you're wondering how I could describe it so accurately, it's because I've been there. People who don't run their own business never understand truly how engrossing it becomes. But I know what it's like to think about your company, staff, and clients, constantly. I think about these things more than anything else. It's insane and nonsensical. But oddly addictive and rewarding. I wrote this book to help you get to the rewarding part faster, or at least, with less of a mental struggle. I'm going to help you and your business navigate this delicate juncture.

Before I delve into the details, I wanted to share something with you. What happened to me at this intersection moment. To keep things as simple as possible, I included the graph below. It's the sales growth of my agency, ramarketing, over the last twelve years. I've circled the point at which I was at my crossroads, where I suspect you are now. You don't need to be a data analyst to get the idea. Importantly, if I was to also draw a graph of my personal growth and sense of fulfilment in life, it would follow this same trajectory.

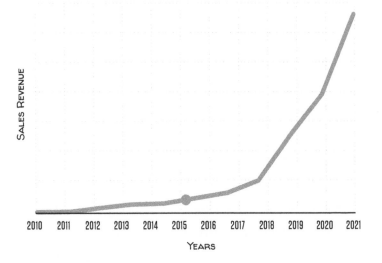

This drastic level of business and personal growth was never actually by design. Simply an outcome of the process I am about to take you through. This may excite you or scare you. Either way, my method will give you choices. You may want to grow your firm as quickly as you can, or you may prefer to cap your size to focus on creating demand. You decide. The point is, there is a way forward that you can deliberately and confidently walk towards. Not only is there a way forward, but it's even better than you could possibly imagine right now. Believe me. I was there and now I'm here.

CHAPTER

1

STOP.
AND BECOME
INTENTIONAL.

t's important to mention that what you're feeling is normal. Don't stress. Imagine you've reached a fork on a hike. You've taken a moment to stop, breathe, and take stock of where you are. You now have a choice. An intentional decision to make. You can opt to keep going without a map and just see where you end up. You can also choose to take a shorter, easier trail that will give you a quicker type of gratification—maybe a nice lake view. Or you could decide to take the harder, longer path that will give you a more fulfilling kind of satisfaction—like a spectacular valley view of six lakes and maybe a breathtaking sunset. The type you will cherish for life, never forget, and not regret. Ahem. You can read between the lines as to which I think you should take.

People like us are rarely satisfied, so the crossing you're contemplating is inevitable. Still, it can catch you by surprise. To fiercely protect, and quite frankly milk, what you have built to date or to push yourself further, find a way to overcome these obstacles and see how far you can take what you have started. This is the founder's frustration. The owner's curse. To balance the cautious, protective, diligent businessperson in us with the progressive, ambitious, entrepreneurial character in us. Both valuable but at times at odds with each other. Quite the quandary.

The problem with the former option here is it seems safer, but it's arguably riskier. It assumes nothing within your control can go wrong. If you keep your head down and keep doing what you're doing, nothing can impact you. It doesn't matter how hard you work and how many hours you put in, you'd be acting naively without even realising it. I chose a variation of option one, the "safe" choice, for the first few years of running my company. I was unintentional about where we were going and just kept working, head down. And then in 2014, our biggest client that represented 35 percent of our revenue went out of business overnight. This client also happened to be my former employer. I was shocked and devastated. Seven years on, it still fills me with sadness.

Fortunately, just before this happened, I begrudgingly attended an event where sales guru Ian Altman was speaking. I say begrudgingly as I was not one for "missing work" to go to a conference. I couldn't possibly justify taking a few hours away from my laptop. What new things did I need to learn? A combination of guilt and arrogance. What a silly sausage I was. But my God, did I learn that day. I wrote so many notes as I learnt about finding the right clients, negotiation, and consultative selling. Little did I know that what I was ferociously absorbing that day would be the catalyst of my business surviving and thriving through the challenge of losing our biggest customer.

The client loss thankfully spurred me into taking stock and getting my shit together. Combined with what I learnt at that event and from Ian's book, *Same Side Selling*, I ultimately adopted many of the steps that enabled me to achieve that fancy curve on the sales graph. The only silver lining of an otherwise awful situation.

I don't want you to find yourself in a similar position to where I was in 2014. I'd rather you get your shit together before the proverbial shit ever hits the fan like it did for me.

I get that you don't want to risk what you have. But if you didn't have an itch you needed to scratch, you probably wouldn't be reading this right now. You're going to grow one way or another. But growth for you and your business can be calm, steady, controlled, and sustainable. Much like you taking the harder, longer hiking path. Sure, this path brings more obstacles, but you don't need to sprint through them. You're in control here. Go at your own pace with a clear plan to achieve a better outcome.

There are no guarantees in life, but you can be intentional. You can make deliberate decisions and adopt the types of behaviours that will give you the best possible chance of achieving the outcome you seek.

It's now time to avoid aimless wandering into a future of regret. To get comfortable with being a little uncomfortable on your path of intentionality. This is the first step in the journey. My hope is that by following this path, it will enable you to live a better, more fulfilled, and successful life. And who doesn't want that?

I do have to warn you: if you're not up for the challenge to do what needs to be done to enhance your life and realise your ambitions, it's best to put this book down. Pick up your smartphone and check your Twitter stream for the millionth time today. Or maybe lose a few hours of your life playing Fruit Ninja or Candy Crush. This is not the book for you.

But if you're the type of person who believes in pushing yourself and living the best life you can, you're in the right place. The remainder of this book will inspire you to take action, and you'll live a better life because you do. Pinky promise.

CHAPTER

2

WIN.
WITH CLARITY.

"Raman, John's on the phone for you…"

This was it. The butterflies were in some kind of uncontrollable tornado spin in the pit of my stomach. John was a potential client at a startup software company, and this was our first phone call after our big pitch. This moment is one of the most nerve-wracking, yet exciting parts of doing what we do. I instantly needed the toilet; I'm not going to lie. All I wanted to know was did we win the deal?

"Hey, Raman. We've decided to go with someone else. You guys did a great job, and we were really impressed with your energy. But someone else knew our industry a little better."

For fuck's sake. Sure, losing a new business opportunity happens to all of us. But when I got this call, it was the third consecutive loss in a matter of weeks. Now, if we'd tried to coast through pitches and do the minimum amount of work, then I'd be cool with the outcome. But we had produced some gorgeous creative designs and a full-blown strategy for all three—a tech company, a charity, and an industrial maritime organisation. And we'd lost all three deals.

I just didn't get it. I had no idea what was going wrong. I was frustrated, angry, and disappointed. This was a head-in-the-hands situation. Imagine a face-palm emoji years before such a thing even existed. Around the same time, we also suffered from a nightmare client project—one that led me to sending the money back to the customer essentially saying, "Go away, please." I just knew something wasn't right in the business. We were still growing, but we were wobbling. And I was feeling overwhelmed and sorry for myself.

The main issue I see with service providers, especially in the early few years, or where there is no clear direction, is a willingness to take on any type of business from any type of client. We were no different. There is little vetting or qualifying of the buyer. You only see the dollar bills and a shiny new client. And that's OK in the early stages, but if you want to get a bit more serious, then you need to know who is the ideal fit.

I can't assume you're at this exact moment right now. It may have already happened to you or might at some point soon. Irrespective, when I arrived at this juncture, it led me to do the type of assessment on my business that I'd never done before. If I'd adopted these practices before, I would not have felt this pain.

So, that's why I have two vital tasks for your business. I will refer to these throughout the book, so please don't be naughty and skip this step!

TASK 1: CREATE A CLIENT MATRIX

First, and most importantly, I'd like you to categorise and plot every one of your existing clients into one of the four boxes in the matrix below. Most service-based businesses like yours will have tens or hundreds of clients rather than thousands, so it should be doable.

Use a twelve-to-eighteen-month time frame to keep it recent and relevant.

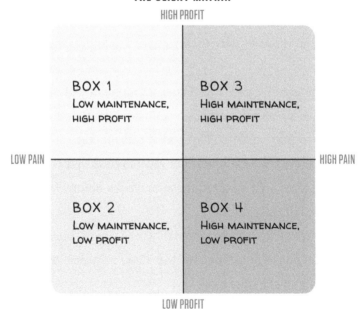

THE CLIENT MATRIX

HIGH PROFIT

LOW PAIN

BOX 1
LOW MAINTENANCE,
HIGH PROFIT

BOX 3
HIGH MAINTENANCE,
HIGH PROFIT

HIGH PAIN

BOX 2
LOW MAINTENANCE,
LOW PROFIT

BOX 4
HIGH MAINTENANCE,
LOW PROFIT

LOW PROFIT

The matrix is simply profit versus pain. It's pretty self-explanatory, but your goal is to identify the nature of your high-profit, low-maintenance clients (in the main) as well as the low-profit, high-maintenance clients who drain the living daylight out of you. You should expect to have a spectrum of client types even within each of the quadrants. Some clients will be right on the edge of a quadrant, and others will be very settled in theirs. Be sure to capture these nuances as you plot.

I'd advise you to start with the good stuff. First, in the top left (Box 1) put the clients that cause you the minimum amount of stress while also making good money. This should give you a real picture of your best buyers. You should adore these people. The type of client that calls and you answer your phone without hesitation.

Next, move to Box 2. Low-pain, low-profit clients are often legacy customers who may have been with you since the early days. Personally, I love these people a lot. You normally have great relationships with them and care about their businesses, and personal relationships may even develop with these people. Some may stay small forever, and some have bags of potential to grow. It's rare that they will leave you. They are often real ambassadors for your business and refer you to others, so they're certainly worth keeping.

Now, onto Box 3. The trickiest category no doubt is the high-maintenance, high-profit ones. These clients often deliver a big chunk to your bottom line (like Box 1) but do so in a painful way. There's no obvious solution for these folks, and they'll be frustrating to no end. Only you will know how important they are to your business and whether the pain is worth it. Based on my experience, I would either work on or invest in making the relationship better. Try identifying the biggest pain points for your team, unrealistic expectations, for example. Share those challenges with the client in an attempt to move them towards Box 1. Or plan for transitioning this client out of the door. Remember, to do that, you'll need a plan to replace the revenue.

And finally, Box 4, the high-maintenance, low-profit customers. Why do you have these clients, please? They make little or no contribution to your business and cause you the maximum number of headaches. The challenging client I mentioned earlier in this chapter fell into this category. The type of client who calls and you hide your phone so you don't have to see their name flashing on your screen. Make a plan to fire these clients. Exiting these relationships will be a huge weight off your shoulders and will free up resources to redeploy to the clients you should be investing your energy in.

By the end of this first task, you will have your client matrix that will resemble the one below.

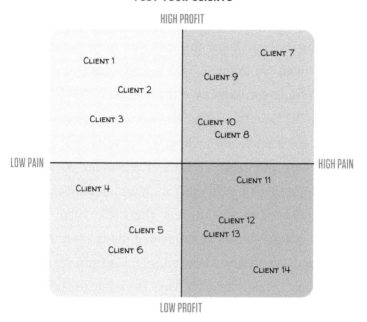

PLOT YOUR CLIENTS

HIGH PROFIT

CLIENT 1
CLIENT 7
CLIENT 9
CLIENT 2
CLIENT 3
CLIENT 10
CLIENT 8

LOW PAIN

HIGH PAIN

CLIENT 4
CLIENT 11
CLIENT 12
CLIENT 5
CLIENT 13
CLIENT 6
CLIENT 14

LOW PROFIT

TASK 2: COMPLETE A LOSS ANALYSIS

Now that you've plotted your clients, I want you to look back at the deals you have lost recently. I had you start with the client matrix to give you context for what is working for you and what you should strive for in the future. So, with a different colour, plot any lost opportunities on the same matrix. If your existing matrix is super cramped already, you can start a new one.

Which of the recent losses do you think would have fit in Box 1 or 2 versus Box 3 or 4? If you're honest with yourself, you'll instinctively know the ones you really would have liked to win. For example, which would have fit into the high-profit, low-maintenance client bucket? Why? Unpack the why. Why was this potential client such a good fit or not? For me, the friendly folks whom we knew we could exceed expectations profitably always win versus the prickly people that I'm not sure we'll ever satisfy, irrespective of money.

As I reflected on the "lost deal" that I talked about at the start of this chapter, all of a sudden it didn't seem that bad a rejection. We were not an agency for startups. We did not know their specific industry. The client didn't really know what they wanted yet and had lofty expectations. And above all, something didn't feel quite right about the company. A big fancy office with very few bodies. Classic style-over-substance tech firm. At best, they would have ended up in Box 2, but more likely Box 4 of our client matrix. Weeks later, John was fired. Within twelve months, the company was out of business. I felt like we had dodged a bullet. It turned out, we had.

PLUS LOST DEALS

HIGH PROFIT

LOW PAIN — | — HIGH PAIN

CLIENT 1
CLIENT 2
CLIENT 3

CLIENT 7
CLIENT 9
LOST DEAL 1
CLIENT 10
CLIENT 8

CLIENT 4
CLIENT 5
LOST DEAL 4
CLIENT 6

CLIENT 11
LOST DEAL 2
CLIENT 12
CLIENT 13
LOST DEAL 3
CLIENT 14

LOW PROFIT

This two-step process can be painful, but you must be brutally honest. Don't sugar-coat the failures or bad decisions as they blind you from truth and opportunity. You can't evolve without learning from your current state of play and the seemingly painful past experiences. By going through this process, you're building a picture—a picture of who is right for your business (today) and who is not. You also want to start visualising how these clients look and feel. I'll talk more about this in the following chapter.

Think of the entire exercise as a treasure hunt that enables you to discover golden clients and poisonous berries. Business life is so much better with the right type of customers. Ultimately, this is the first step in making you a better, leaner, more impactful business.

This analysis is intentionally simple. It doesn't require an MBA. But therein lies your advantage as a scrappy entrepreneur. It'll take you a day or two (max) and give you 80 percent of the insight you need without reading fifty business analysis books or spending $100,000. You're so very welcome! ;)

After these tasks, I want you to feel like you are seeing patterns or getting a greater sense of clarity. When I did this at my crossroads moment (remember the fancy graph?), only fifteen of our thirty clients were in the right boxes. None of the deals we recently lost were actually as brilliant a fit as I thought. Plus, the gut-wrenching client project we'd experienced had given me a stark dose of understanding that every client is not a good client. So, I started to see where we needed to focus our efforts. Whether you're at the start of your journey or twenty years in, by the end of this process, I suspect you will too.

CHAPTER

3

FOCUS.
FIND YOUR NICHE.

'm hoping Chapter 2 has helped you discover your true treasure: that 20–40 percent of clients who are actually generating 80 percent of your profit, ideally without the hassle and headache of the remaining clients.

When I did this back in 2015, I realised that although we serviced about eight different sectors, the top performers that we loved working with were actually from just two sectors. In fact, the vast majority of these were from one industry. I'd never analysed our customer data in such a methodical manner. I wish I had. I would have reached my epiphany much sooner.

Seeing the data plotted so simply felt like putting contact lenses into my eyes. The blur became clear. The fuzzy fog lifted. I could see the trail ahead. I knew where to go to play our game and who we wanted to play with. I felt a greater sense of clarity, calm, and confidence about who we should exist to serve and who we should not exist to serve. The clients who truly appreciated who we were and what we did for them. This, if you like, was my eureka moment. I remember feeling genuinely excited when this happened but also a bit annoyed that I'd not come to this realisation before.

Following this penny-dropping point, we selected one sector where we already had a good track record (drug development service providers), and a sector where we were seeing potential (automotive service providers). Both broadly under the umbrella of industrial supply chains. Sexy, I know. The reality is the common thread between them—both B2B, highly technical, regulated, and global—was where we thrived in partnerships. At the time, 50 percent of our business was B2C or non-industrial (primarily Boxes 3 and 4 in our client matrix). This is where the bulk of the hassle was and where we struggled to consistently win new clients and grow existing ones. As difficult as it was to stomach, I knew it was the beginning of the end for a big chunk of our existing business. But I also felt the potential of the other markets. It's almost like I could see the route I wanted to take for the business, but I had to overcome some obstacles before we could be free to roam in that desired direction.

I can sense your nervousness. You're probably thinking, how on earth could we possibly just solely focus on less than half of our clients? Also, how niche do we go? This is where sector selection or some other core buyer commonality (e.g., buyer type, location, size of business) is really important. My suggestion is to go as micro and specific as possible to start with, and then you can always expand from that point into complementary areas.

Do not think this means you have to put all your eggs in one basket on day one. Rather, this is the moment to be frank with yourself, to realise that unless you're Apple, Google, or Amazon, "the world" is not your target. Trying to be everything to everyone led me and my team somewhere I did not want to be—stuck. The same outcome is inevitable for most. Focus will save you a lot of frustration and heartbreaking loss. The exercises I've outlined will sharpen your focus and keep you from chasing the wrong type of customers, getting distracted, and ultimately lost.

Remember, there's always time to extend and expand your talents, reputation, and resources into adjacent areas. Let's say you could choose to service personal injury law firms locally to build up your client base, track record, and expertise. When you feel you have maxed that niche, you can evolve to another area of law or a wider geographic area. The value is in your knowledge of the niche.

If we purely just think about sectors for a moment, there are over 150 industries listed on LinkedIn. Within each of those, there are multiple sub-segments. What I would not advise you to do is try to focus on a completely new sector that you have no experience in or that has a high barrier to entry that you are not qualified to do. For example, aerospace may seem like a high-value, global sector, but it won't be easy to crack quickly, especially if you need to cover half of your revenue from firing bad client fits.

Instead, start with the low-hanging fruit. The sector you can smash out of the park that is already heavily represented in your client matrix. If you're an SEO firm with retail experience and great clients in this space, chase new online retail clients. If you're a designer with a profitable portfolio in education, focus on those buyers exclusively for the next year. You get the picture.

Go back to the data from the previous chapter. Turn your attention specifically to Boxes 1 and 2. Where are you super strong and where do you feel there is real potential? You have a competitive edge for this audience already. That's a leap of faith worth taking. Faith with tangible evidence.

Next, think about what you offer or can offer this attractive and receptive audience you have identified better than anyone else. You want to become so irresistible to this audience that you are simply too awesome to overlook. To help you, answer this question: "What's the one thing that your firm can offer to this audience that is truly world-class?"

You might be able to answer this question straight away. But for others, it will be a head-scratcher, and that's fine. Whether you are world-class now is not the point. This is about unlocking the capabilities you need to excel in order to meet the needs of your ideal customers better than anyone else. Put another way, this is your domain expertise.

Combining craftsmanship with your sector specialism. A customer experience specialist for premium car dealerships. A GDPR training expert for SaaS companies. An engineering technician for railroad clients. You get the idea. That's your sweet spot right there. See below:

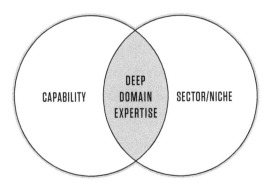

Back in 2015, we were primarily a media communications and content agency for the life science space. We used this sweet spot to attract clients and then smash projects out of the park. Our clients loved us, trusted us, and wanted more. So, we added design, digital, web, and more disciplines to become a full-service marketing agency to the market we served. Being world-class at the PR piece was what gave us traction and market credibility. We subsequently evolved that into a comprehensive marketing service for our niche audience.

What is your PR piece? What's the combination of audience need and capability magnificence that will be like honey to a bee?

Let's say market research is your thing and you're focusing on the banking sector. This overlap of expertise and industry knowledge is your superpower. Now, use that as the tempting bait to attract and win new clients. Then, wow the bloody hell out of them, which will open new doors and opportunities for you to support their efforts. Notice I'm not saying up-sell or cross-sell. Focus on simply adding value to your clients by solving the problems they tell you about, and they'll buy other offerings your business has. Even better, they will tell other people across the same industry. As the sensational Seth Godin says, "It's about becoming *meaningfully specific to the smallest viable audience.*" Giving the client the sense that you actually exist for them, because you know their pain, how they feel, and how to solve that issue.

Let's say you damage your knee jumping with excitement after reading my book. Sorry about that. You call the doctor's office, and you have two options.

1. You can see a general medical practitioner, and it will cost $100.

2. Or you can see a knee specialist that deals with jumping-related knee injuries every day, but it will cost you $200.

I'm 99 percent certain you will go for the latter, even at twice the price. At the most fundamental level, that's the value of a specialist. Their specific knowledge makes them more valuable. The higher price intrinsically attaches more value to the buyer too.

So who do you know inside and out? Who is your audience that will pay double for your specialism? If you can't think of an answer right away, try to imagine who you would pay double to help you. For us, we use an accountancy firm for our business that specialises in UK and US accounting and tax. I'm pretty sure they are two times the cost of what we used to pay for our previous partner. And do I care? Absolutely not. The confidence and reassurance we get from someone who knows the complexity, rules, and regulations of the UK–US tax treaty is more than worth it. Once you know the kind of niche solution you're looking for in a business partner, you can start to understand what it is you offer others, and the value of this is amplified.

As you look for your specific world-class offering, try not to put too much pressure on yourself. Your decision will evolve as your team changes and grows. Just remember, the more niche the better at the start. Don't follow the crowd—if everyone is trying to fit through one door, go for another one. We opted to focus on one sector that we could attack confidently right away and another one that was more exploratory. We took what felt like a massive risk at the time (which in hindsight I wish I had done many years earlier) to be purposeful, relevant, and compelling for 0.01 percent of the world. Put another way, we became invisible to most and unmissable to those who needed us most. This can feel uncomfortable as many "won't get it." But you don't exist for the many.

One of the biggest added benefits of going through this process is the operational clarity it delivers once you know where to focus. Up to this point, I suspect your business development, recruitment, marketing materials, messaging, and training have all been quite general. Likely, you simply did what seemed important in the moment and went with the flow, without much foresight or specificity. But trying to be everything to everyone leads to generality, exhausting client relationships, and a lot of lost business. No one wins. Once you have this narrower field of vision, everything else narrows, in a good way. The events you attend, the people you recruit, the types of clients you target, the language you use on your website, and the media you consume will all now be embedded in your focus areas. Believe me, this is a much smarter, leaner, and productive way of running a growing service business.

By applying these constraints, you learn to maximise and excel in the limited space you have to play. It's like spending years trying to master several instruments, then eventually opting to focus on the one you're most passionate about and actually good at. Magic appears from attempting such mastery.

CHAPTER

4

EVOLVE.
AND GET YOUR HOUSE IN ORDER.

"Oh, ignore our website. It's been on our list to update it for ages. We've not had the chance to update it in a while. We don't even offer that service anymore." If I received a dollar for every time I've heard this from owners of service providers just like you. It's especially ironic coming from marketing firms.

For my fellow marketing mates, it's like being a hairstylist with damaged hair and the worst haircut in the world. Or a tax accountant who has lost all his receipts and missed his tax return deadline. Or a personal trainer with high blood pressure and a huge belly. You get the point.

Don't be that person, please. You're better than that. You've been following my guide up until this point, so I know you're not afraid of some serious effort, courage, and soul searching; so good on you. Carry that into the way you interact with and serve your clients. Seamlessness all comes down to alignment, internally and externally. Practising what you preach. Creating a consistent identity, both inside and outside.

By now, you should have a good idea of the audience you're going to focus on serving going forward and what they value from you. But I want you to get a little more granular with your customer. "We target procurement people who work for automotive companies" is not specific enough. The more precise you can get with the person you have to wow, the better. You should be able to describe the particulars of these people and exactly how you can solve their specific problems better than others, in intricate details. This is something worth obsessing over in your business. To help, I have three key tasks for you.

TASK 1: TAKE YOUR TEAM ON THE JOURNEY

If you're feeling excited by the direction you're headed and are raring to go, that's marvellous. But take a second. Before you start changing everything and refocusing on specific market segments, you need to ensure your team (even if you have a small one) understands why this is happening and buys into the pivot you're making. The decision is made in your mind, but this may be a monumental move for your business and might not be for everyone. You need to inform them, explain it, and get them involved.

How are you going to do this? First, make sufficient time to brief them, and then discuss and invite feedback. Sending an email to everyone is not how to communicate a seismic shift in how you want to position and transform the business in the future.

When I did this, I took several of my key colleagues offsite and we had dinner together at a painstakingly trendy bowling alley burger joint. There were six of us, plus my two mentors and an external business associate whom I highly respect. Around that time, I had read the brilliant book *Legacy* by James Kerr that chronicles the culture of the legendary New Zealand All Blacks rugby team. It's about setting the highest standards but conducting yourself in a respectful, dignified way. I brought lots of these learnings into my visual presentation that was intended to inspire, excite, and create a very clear picture of where we would be heading. I approached it like I was doing a keynote speech to hundreds. It all felt special, important, and compelling.

I declared that one day, we would be drinking cocktails at a rooftop bar in Tokyo, Japan. A vision the team could genuinely visualise, feel, and aim towards. The point was that we would be a truly global business one day and that our reputation would be so good that we'd managed to work with a Japanese pharmaceutical company. A very conservative industry in an equally as conservative business culture. Clearly, it would not happen overnight. It would require patience, dedication to the industry, and the production of consistently good work over many years. Nevertheless, our North Star was clear.

What's interesting is when I made the decision to specialise my agency, the general consensus from the team was that we should remain a generalist to keep things more varied and interesting. Importantly, for *them* rather than our clients. It might have been better for their careers to have a broader selection of client types to work on. But that motivation was not in the interests of our business. The irony, of course, were those who adapted and endured the growth have seen their careers propel at a velocity that would never have happened otherwise.

This could happen to you too, so you need to be headstrong and believe in what you're doing. I compromised with my team and said 80 percent of what we do will be niche-focused and we can keep 20 percent for the supposed "fun" stuff. That never really materialised. After six months, the momentum of the former bulldozed the non-core stuff into rubble. All of a sudden, we were on a rocket ship. Not many wanted to get off, other than the ones who did not want to handle the pace, which was fine. Interestingly, if the clients we had in 2015 were the same when COVID-19 arrived, we would have gone out of business. Clearly, none of us had that foresight, but nevertheless, I'm so grateful we made that tough call and that the bulk of the team followed me on the journey.

Just beware; you may lose people. We did and I was fine with it. The direction you are now headed is not what some of your team bought into when they originally joined, so you have to respect and address this. But the ones who don't depart become walking, talking ambassadors for what you're trying to achieve. And that is magical to see. The energy plus traction is infectious.

TASK 2: BLUEPRINT YOUR BEST BUYER

If a new person started in your business tomorrow and asked exactly who you target, would you be able to show them? I'm sure you could explain it, but would it be clearly documented? And if the newbie then asked one of your colleagues, would they get exactly the same answer? I suspect not. There should be a clear and consistent answer to this question from anyone and everyone in your firm. But it won't happen by accident.

This task is about discussing, agreeing, and recording exactly who your business exists to serve, hence the idea of creating a blueprint for everyone to understand and follow for the future. It's another task to do in collaboration with your team as it specifically focuses on your ideal buyers. At this brainstorm stage, literally sketch the details on a piece of paper or a whiteboard. Capture all the little details you can refine later. "Draft ugly, edit pretty," as Neil Strauss says.

The chances are, you'll already have some of these buyers as existing clients. Look back at your client matrix and, in particular, Box 1. Pay very close attention to the high-profit, low-maintenance section. In addition, don't overlook the low-profit, low-maintenance clients in Box 2. These folks often have bags of potential and tend to be very loyal, long-term buyers that sometimes graduate into Box 1.

As you start to develop a clearer blueprint of the right buyers for your organisation, you'll begin to notice themes in your client base. You might notice similarities, such as functional things like company size, location, revenue, number of employees, etc. (The fancy marketing word for this is firmographics.) But you will also cover demographics (typical age, gender, education, role, etc.) and behavioural aspects, like benefits sought, expectation levels versus previous providers, etc. All the information in your initial blueprints enables you to develop a crystal clear picture of your best buyers, which you can turn into what we call a buyer persona, i.e., a more robust, documented client profile of the people you exist to help and that will appreciate (and hopefully adore) your organisation.

By the end of the process, you'll have a few profiles of your ideal customers documented, especially if you are looking at a few different sectors. Within each target customer, you may also have a couple of different key stakeholders who are involved in buying the expertise you provide, e.g., a gatekeeper (who might find your firm in the first place) and then the main "boss" decision maker (that holds the budget pot and rubber stamps the final decision). Make sure you do this exercise for each of your specific buyers.

The final blueprint should look like the example below.

SIMPLE BUYER PERSONA TEMPLATE

NAME

JOB TITLE

COMPANY PROFILE

DECISION ROLE

WHAT DO WE KNOW ABOUT THEM?

GOALS AND CHALLENGES
What is the goal here?
What challenge are they trying to overcome?

EMPATHY
What are the pain points?
How are they feeling?

DECISION MAKING
Who else is involved in the decision?
Who do they need to impress?

PERCEPTIONS
How do they identify and search for a company like ours?
How do they view us and/or our competition?

HERO ROLE
How can we help them overcome these challenges and be their hero?
What would success look and feel like?

BENEFITS
What rational benefits do we offer?
What emotional benefits do we offer?

Again, don't forget to include your team in this exercise. You can even use an external facilitator to help run a workshop to work through this important task. If you're unfamiliar with the process, it may seem like a lot of work, but crafting thorough blueprints to create these personas as soon as possible will provide the focus you need to get unstuck. Your future self will thank you for having done this immediately and thoroughly.

Not only will your existing team all have a solid and consistent understanding of your customers, but this knowledge will then transfer to any new people who join the business. Name your personas (often after existing clients), and they will become common language in your business as you grow, helping keep clients front and centre. We have Colin, Denise, Aimee, and Alison. Each overlap slightly but has specific needs and wants. All are based on real-life clients in our business, so they feel human and tangible.

TASK 3: REFINE YOUR MARKETING MESSAGES

Armed with your learnings and discussions from the previous two steps, make sure your marketing materials and messages evolve to reflect the needs of these buyers. You are not a store for everyone. A catch-all approach may increase the web traffic and inbound enquiry count, but it's also burning your resource on the wrong type of opportunities. Be very clear about who you exist for and what you can do better than others for the person who actually cares. Remember, your goal is to be unmissable by the people who need you. The only way to do that is with very clear language and relevant solutions.

If you're going to be pitching yourself as a design specialist for the fintech sector, then make sure the language, imagery, and messaging around your brand reflect this. You'll confuse your market if they hit your website and it looks like you're a generalist design firm and fintech is buried somewhere within your website. Again, this is not rocket science. Always be speaking to the needs, thoughts, and pains of your buyer and not all about you.

You may be reading this and thinking, *Well, this is obvious*. And you're right, it is. But believe me, I've seen so many businesses like yours miss this vital step. Not sort their own hair. Not complete their own tax return on time. Not look after their own health. Often, not practice what they preach. This process is about really defining who you exist for and then redefining what you want the world to see. Sometimes, you have to start slow to go fast, so don't skip this step. It's also putting your stake in the ground internally and externally in a robust manner, which requires courage and brings accountability.

Let me illustrate the value of this process. After we decided to pivot the focus of the business, I outlined the vision. Then together with my team, we sketched blueprints and created our buyer personas.

Our messaging evolved from a slightly generic catch-all:

"We can help [any] company raise their brand profile..."

to a much more specific and resonating message:

"If you're responsible for marketing in a clinical manufacturing business, we can help raise your brand's profile in the pharmaceutical sector..."

Chalk and cheese, right? If you were a marketing lead in a clinical manufacturing business, which would appeal to you? Exactly. All this thought, input, and focus leads to a much more piercing and meaningful output.

After we went through this process, I always recall an enquiry we got from a potential client. When we spoke to her, she said, "*I cannot believe an agency like yours exists. Someone that's in the weeds of my industry every day and knows the jargon.*"

She was literally giddy with excitement. Like we existed *just* for her. Because we did and do. They became a client within weeks, and that was four years ago. They were a low-profit, low-maintenance client for the first few years, but also referred us to a major new client. They have since transitioned to a high-profit, low-maintenance client who now spends hundreds of thousands of dollars with us each year. This could never have happened without going through the above. It also reinforces the value of not dismissing the potential of clients that are in Box 2 of your matrix that are a good fit. To this day, I obsess with the specific terminology we use in our marketing materials so our potential clients can identify with the problems they are facing and how we solve them.

It's funny, because even as a marketing person, this felt like a lot of effort at the time. But moments like that conversation reminded me why the effort matters. It's actually remarkable when those ideal clients you have documented come knocking on your door. Even as a consumer, I'm sure you've experienced the moment where you're sure a company or brand exists just for you. Clothing brands with garments that fit you perfectly. A hipster beer store that you can spend all day in. A make-up brand that beautifully works with your skin tone. It's equally as magical a feeling for a customer to feel such a connection. Get it right and it's a glorious feeling for everyone.

As your business evolves, never ever stop giving a damn about who you exist for and how this audience sees you. Always be in touch with your customers' wants and needs, as they will shift over time. It's always a work in progress and never definitive. This is one of the reasons I speak to our clients all the time. I might not be delivering all the work like I did a few years ago, but I am constantly morphing our business to what they need. You need to do the same. Ask questions, listen, look for patterns, and adapt your offering.

With a clear vision about what you offer and to exactly whom, you and your team can shift your efforts towards becoming the best in your field. The best marketing trick in the business is simply focusing on your service experience. It's what you learn on day one in a marketing lesson. The first P of the marketing mix is product. Your product is the services you deliver. So, work relentlessly at improving your service capability and building your reputation. Be consistently great. Nothing is more powerful than a solid niche reputation. Word spreads quickly in any industry vertical.

My final suggestion here is to become an educator and helpful resource in the space you've carved out for yourself. Give away content, share ideas, and offer insights. Make sure your business is generous to your target audience, and they will appreciate, value, respect, and, ultimately, trust you. Plus, when they're in the buying cycle, needing to find someone to fix the exact problem you live to solve, guess what? They'll probably knock on your door. No hard sell will be required because they've already bought into your expertise. In fact, on the day I write this, a potential client has contacted me purely on the basis of attending our free webinars and listening to my sector-specific podcast. No selling, yelling, or telling. Just helping in a relevant manner.

If you're going to get your house in order, then do it properly. No shortcuts. Lean into it as it's enjoyable. Put in the hard yards now so you'll reap the benefits for many years ahead. I'm not going to lie, I'm excited for you right now.

CHAPTER

5

SAY NO.
BUILD A DEFENCE SYSTEM.

As my wife and I drove our kids to the doctor's office in Boston to get their annual flu shots, my five-year-old son was petrified by the thought of a needle stabbing his arm. The little guy's curious nature led him to ask me why he even needed one. To my wife's surprise (given she is a medical doctor), I managed to explain it to him in words he understood. I said that getting this injection was like creating an invisible shield around his body. If any bad bugs try to get in, this little army was there all day, every day to fight them off and protect him. All of a sudden, the shot became less daunting to my kids in the context of having their very own army to protect them.

In much the same way a flu shot protects my family, you need to proactively build a defence system to protect your business from bad clients who can find their way into your organisation, infect your culture, and make you seriously sick. This is about saying no. Turning down enquiries. Rejecting new business opportunities.

Surely, you can't say no to a pile of cold hard cash, right? Well, erm, you can. And you may have to get used to it. The truth is, most business will not be right for you once you've identified your specific niche focus areas, and that can feel very weird at the start. When you've spent several years welcoming every opportunity with open arms, saying no seems unimaginable. I learnt this back in 2014 in Ian Altman's tremendous book, *Same Side Selling*, where he talks about "forcing the fit," and that's precisely what you need to stop doing. Trying to force prospects that are not a good fit for you into clients is the classic square pegs, round holes.

Up to this point, we've intentionally focused on who is the right fit. But now we're going to address the pesky people in Boxes 3 and 4 of your client matrix. The ones causing you the most stress for the littlest return. It's with them in mind that we will create a list of the kinds of characteristics and behaviours from clients that you don't want moving forward.

Take a moment and think about these nightmare projects and client relationships. What was it about the client, nature of the project, industry, or anything that contributed to a less-than-satisfactory outcome? Put simply, if you had the chance to do the project again, you'd say no in a heartbeat.

I learnt this the hard way, many years ago, before we had done any of the exercises I've outlined so far. Typically for the time, I was blinded by the "big city" location of the business, a charming client, and the promise of potential future business and network referrals. In reality, the client had the budget for an old Toyota Corolla and was expecting a brand-new Ferrari. The signs were there early on, but I had the blinders on. Unrealistic demands. Minuscule budget. Misalignment of expectations. Calls out of office hours insisting on speaking to me. I recall it being a very stressful time that quickly spilt into my home life. I actually feel a little queasy thinking about it now! An awful experience. It was so disastrous that I eventually called the client to say I had transferred all the money back to them and wished them the best. They were not horrible, bad people. Just a terrible fit.

The aftermath of this project was like a post-mortem. What the fuck just happened here? Along with my account manager and designer, we sat solemnly at a table and unpacked everything. From start to finish, we left no stone unturned. After an honest look at our process, we saw that as a team, we skipped the pre-qualifications, we didn't scope correctly, or even ask whether this was the right fit for us to begin with. Looking back now, it was so unbelievably naive, but to this day, one of the best lessons I've ever had in business.

Learning from these painful experiences will help you prevent these people from ever entering your business in the first place. Head them off at the pass before they terrorise you. Imagine your business like a nightclub, and you're the head doorman: "Sorry, guys, you're not getting in tonight. Or ever, in fact." This is about building your defence system. Getting your own little army ready to protect you from infection.

It wasn't all bad, however. One good thing that resulted from our awful experience was a checklist for our internal team. It's more than an assessment. It's our flu shot for each potential client. It works to defend us from any potential hazards. Here are five examples of what's on our checklist that you can adopt:

1. Are they the type of people we want to work with? If they are not, it's not worth it. Even last week, my colleague took a call from a fast-growing pharmaceutical business in Europe that, on the face of it, looked like a great fit. But my colleague said the potential client was arrogant, a bit offensive, and just not nice. Easy decision. See you later, pal. Even if it's a perfect sector fit, a bad client can cost you a lot more than the revenue they contribute.

2. Asking for a proposal or information within a ridiculous time frame, without them giving you enough (or any) time or input. These people are fishing, don't respect your expertise, or value what you do. Walk away.

3. Assuming lots of additional items are also included in the project you have outlined, even though they're

clearly not. This will not be a fair and reasonable client. For example, we had a client once who commissioned us to design a corporate brochure. That's it. Nice and simple, right? When the project started, the client then asked when we'd be doing a photography shoot and interviewing the team for content, despite the fact neither had been discussed! Lesson learnt for us...never assume and always ask about these things upfront. More often than not, it's not malicious, but just a lack of knowledge on the client's part. But there are some cheeky chancers out there, so watch out!

4. Unwarranted stressing and chasing for no apparent reason. We saw this a lot in our early days. Clients would pass the pressure buck back to our team, even though the issues were their own internal challenges. This behaviour is usually more of a habit and will become a continuous theme for you, should you take them on as a client. Beware.

5. A sense that this person is an energy-sucking vampire who will cause our team a world of pain. Get your trainers on and run away. Quickly.

Developing the ability to quickly identify what a bad client looks like is equally as important as the ability of spotting a good one. But saying no to business takes courage. It will happen more as you transition towards your sweet spot focus area. But, as you win more of the right clients and let go of the others, your confidence will grow.

One of the positive side effects is that saying no feels exhilarating and empowering. It also stops you from wasting time, money, and resources. You may also end up referring work to others, which is always nice. If you're a firm of architects who solely specialises in the offshore energy sector, and you get an enquiry for a local retailer wanting to design a new store, then politely say no and pass it to someone else who will knock it out of the park. It's generous, and everyone is a winner. Many people choose to monetise this via referral agreements. I simply believe in karma. Help others and others will help you. It's worked well for me, for which I'm very grateful.

But what happens when you get an opportunity that you know is not a good fit, but the client is armed with a briefcase full of cash? Quite simply, don't chase the money. Particularly in the early days of running any business, it's hard to turn down cash. But, once you have a firm handle on who your ideal client is and how to wow them, you cannot get distracted by other opportunities...especially if it's just for money. Not all clients will be good clients. You already know this. And if it doesn't feel right, it's probably not. Always ask yourself, "Is this really going to be worth it?" If you're even asking this question, that's a red flag right there. Add that to your defence system.

Like a tantalizing chocolate cake on a healthy day, you must try to resist and walk away. Have faith that there is a better opportunity around the corner. Stick to your guns and play the long game. Try to be rational and do not ignore your instinct. You'll regret it. Keep laser focused on attracting and working on projects that are the right fit and where you are super confident of making an impact. And the money takes care of itself.

Chasing the money generally as you grow leads to daft decisions, often driven by greed and not common sense. It's like going fruit picking, which I did with my kids recently. You get a little bag to fill with delicious, ripe fruit. And when your bag is brimming with, say, sumptuous berries, you shoehorn a few big but slightly mouldy-looking apples. And guess what? The fungus spreads to the rest of your fruit. It all feels yucky, and the bag just gets too heavy to carry. And you drop the lot. Beware of these bad apples as you're always the one left picking up the pieces. All in the name of a little extra. Was it really worth it?

I get it, though. It's not as easy as it sounds. And I've not followed my own advice at times and made this mistake. There are opportunities we've undertaken that we shouldn't have. The difficulty as an owner is you have wages to pay and bills to cover, which makes it really hard to reject a project that is going to make a financial impact. There will be a time when you're faced with a "take this project or risk losing someone in your team" situation. Yuk.

Sometimes the green is just too good to walk away from despite all the warning signs and alarms going off in your defence system. This can be particularly challenging if you're going through a lean patch, and the pressure is on to convert and win a new piece of business. Your mind can be very powerful in persuading you, *this* one is different. *This* one will be worth it. Right, I'm sure it will be. My only advice if you opt to take the briefcase of bills despite your better judgment is to set very clear expectations up front with the client in terms of scope, deliverables, ways of working, and what is not included. This will protect you to a certain extent, but make sure there is an option to eject, like a break clause.

If you do the above diligently, consistently, and hold your nerve in the face of tempting opportunities, you'll get more of the type of work you want to do, and your conversion rate will go through the roof. What happens when you start saying no is you also spot the yes opportunities instantly. From the tone of the enquiry, the job title of the person, the language they use, their project needs, etc. You will instinctively know it's a persona that is the right fit for you. What's more, you've now got the time to give the right opportunity the right level of attention it deserves. You can then give these your all. Unsurprisingly, you will secure clients aligned to your business' strategy that will ultimately help your company go in the direction you want and give you a solid foundation for sustainable growth.

So don't chase the opportunities that are not right for your business. You don't need to get every client. You just need the ones who get you. I will leave you with a line from the wonderful Derek Sivers that sums this up perfectly: "If it's not a hell yeah, it's a no."

CHAPTER

6

MONEY.
MAKE IT,
DON'T CHASE IT.

So, I've just told you *not* to chase money. And now I'm going to tell you to *make* money. It's not a contradiction, I promise. Hear me out.

Many years ago, when I was first starting out, my cousin, Rubi, sent me an article on something called the law of obliquity. He tore it out of a magazine and put it in the post. God, I'm old. The author, John Kay, talked about obliquity as the principle that complex goals are best achieved indirectly. I remember reading this article (and I was not exactly one for reading back in the early days) with a learning that money could not be my goal. I remember reaching a realisation that if I focused on a handful of important aspects in my business, then money would be a likely, indirect by-product.

If you just chase the money as your sole goal, it will never be enough. If cash is always the driver of your success, then you'll always desire more. When you make $10,000, you'll then want to make $20,000. And when you make $100,000, you'll want to make $200,000. It will never end. By focusing on doing the right things for your clients and your team, the money will come. The irony in my own experience is that my business has probably achieved far more "moneywise" than I ever would have dreamed of or set as a goal back then.

Money is such a taboo subject, right? How much do you earn? How much did you make last year? What did that cost?

You can see people visibly wince when asked these kinds of questions. Everyone has a different view on money and applies a different value. You might be extremely motivated by money. You might just see it as a marker for success. And others might just see it being an outcome of the good work they do. Whatever your relationship to or view of money, there's some lessons I've learnt on my journey that I hope will help you on yours.

Whether you're still relatively new to running your own firm or you're a decade in, I suspect you're already making better money now than you were before you took the brave step. This is one of the best things about being a skilled expert. You can sell that expertise to those who really need and value it, without the extra overhead costs that other companies deal with.

My first and most important piece of advice here is simple: make money. Every month if you can. I know that's easier said than done, but service businesses like yours should not be breaking even or taking a loss. Assuming you don't have a finance specialist in your team, simply go through your numbers with a fine-tooth comb. Keep it simple. Assess what's coming in and what's going out. Where are you wasting money with unnecessary spend? I'd suggest asking your accountant to help if possible. If you are not making money, you either don't have enough business or the right type of business. Your costing or pricing might be off. Maybe your overhead expenses have crept up without you realising. You might simply be carrying too many bodies. Whatever the causes, identify them, and break any bad habits now.

Making money in an expertise-based business is doable in month one if you have a paying client. In a post-COVID-19 world, we are very used to working from home and utilising the technology available. I'm not saying you don't need an office, but client expectations are very different in this new, smaller, virtually connected world. So, if you can save the office cost and opt for the remote model (strangely, what we did 2009–2013), go for it. It's much easier to make money without this overhead.

My business has made money pretty much every month in twelve years. I'm very loud and proud about that. For me, I remember the company bank balance just going up and up. I never took much money out of the business in the early days, so it almost felt like an out-of-body experience thinking wow, look at all that money. Almost removed from the fact that it was pretty much mine. Having a healthy bank balance gives you a comforting feeling if you have self-doubt (like I did) or decide to take what feels like a risky move.

The next thing I'd advise is to pay yourself properly. It took me seven years to figure this out for myself. Year *seven*. Insane, right? That year, we hired a person who had a salary that was £30,000 higher than what I made. My fellow director was not happy about this and literally made me pay myself market rate. My approach prior to this was to give myself a modest salary and then take money off the table when I really needed it. The reason I did this was to keep as much cash in the business as possible so I didn't have to borrow any money and could invest in what the business needed (software, people, equipment, etc.) without ever really thinking and stressing about it. Also, I didn't really *need* the money and was just risk-averse. To be honest, I have always done this, but now I am paid a "proper" market rate salary. It therefore provides a truer reflection of how the business is performing. Paying yourself an unrealistically low salary may boost your profit line, but you're actually distorting the numbers if your market rate is £80,000 and you're paid £30,000. In addition, at some point I realised there was a difference between the salary I was paid for delivering in my day job and the profits I made for owning the business (and carrying the risk). They are two different things.

So, if you're not already, pay yourself properly, without starving the company of cash. Don't be overly lavish or flashy, but recognise your own contribution. Ask yourself, if you were to take your professional skill and experience somewhere else, what would they pay you? Whatever you choose as your remuneration, it should be higher than this figure. You're not just paid for your technical skill but for leading the business.

That leads me nicely on to company cash. One thing I did from day one was create separate bank accounts, so I physically separated any tax money or business savings from the day-to-day running of the business. There is a terrific book called *Profit First* that I'd highly recommend. The book talks about "always be making money" and not falling into the trap of adding more costs that ultimately impact your bottom line. In an entrepreneurial twist on conventional accounting, it guides you in how to achieve the profit you want by working bottom-up, rather than top-down (i.e., starting with sales, expenses, and profit). It also has some great tips on how to allocate cash, building a frugal mindset in your business, and finding hidden money in your business.

We did a version of what this book advises from the very beginning, without ever knowing it. I've seen so many companies get into trouble by spending every penny they make in sales only to be hit with a tax bill they can't afford. I feared this outcome from day one. So, as risky and courageous as I seem with my business, I'm cautious with cash. We always "over-save" just in case. This goes back to having a sustainable business that can last the test of time. Always having money in the bank gives you peace of mind.

One of the intriguing challenges you begin to face as your business evolves is you have more money to play with. And like anything in life, when you have more money, there is a tendency to buy more, buy bigger, and buy better stuff. Even if your role moves away from the day-to-day numbers, keep a close eye on what is going out of your business. You will be able to sniff out any wastage quicker than anyone. Use this superpower of yours to conserve cash and also make your team understand how important it is not to be wasteful. I often ask my team, "Would you spend your own money on this?" Ninety percent of the time, it's a no.

I'm Indian. So, I feel like I have a natural advantage over most when it comes to doing a deal, negotiating a discount, and being a little thrifty. It's literally in my DNA. But having a frugal and resourceful mindset will make you and your team more innovative and creative. I guarantee it. Chucking money at things is rarely the answer. There are exceptions, like the hires you make, the working environment for your team, and systems that make you more efficient. I'm not saying cut corners. Go big where you need to go big. Where you will get the greatest return for your investment. For me, staff welfare is one of these things. I don't think you should ever be cheap on this, as it's why people stay with a company and give their all. Because they feel (and are) truly valued and cared for. Simple things like good coffee, free snacks, team lunches, and Friday beers cost very little in the grand scheme of things but mean a lot to your team. As my company has matured, we've also added benefits like healthcare, pension, and life insurance that become more valuable as life progresses.

Does the thought of being responsible for people's mortgages and rent not worry you? Honestly, I've never once worried about this like you hear others talking about. Why? Because we've made money and saved cash. The incomings are always more than the outgoings. It's as simple as that. If your business is struggling to do this (other than when you're in a particular phase of investment), then something is wrong. You're selling people, time, and expertise, not products that have a raw material cost attached. Sorry to sound like a broken record, but there is no excuse. Even if you're not motivated by money, your business should still be consistently generating a profit. What you decide to do with that money is your call. Irrespective, get your business into the habit of just being profitable.

I'm a big believer in lean operations, just like a food diet. I manage and monitor what goes in and out. Binge diets rarely work. Like huge cost cuts or big splurges. Instead, opt for a consistently moderate, balanced, and healthy diet. And when you want to splurge and have a cheat weekend, you can, without any major repercussions. Sustainable, gradual, profitable growth—that should be the aim. It also gives you the solid foundation to scale up if, as, or when you need to.

I'll end this chapter with a little story and lesson about pricing as a specialist. The first-ever international project we won was with a Danish pharmaceutical manufacturing company back in 2014. We put everything we had into the pitch to win the job. I recall the project value being about £15,000, which was huge for us at the time. It was a monumental moment in our journey. I distinctly remember being on the plane to Denmark with two colleagues in disbelief this was happening. I am travelling internationally "for work" and someone else is paying for it. Unbelievable.

When we met the client and kicked off the project, I was able to begin building a relationship with our buyer. I asked him why he chose us over the other agencies. He explained that he loved our specialism and knowledge of the pharmaceutical manufacturing space. He then smiled slightly with a raised eyebrow and said we almost lost the project. Naturally, I enquired why.

He said, "You were so much cheaper than the alternative. Yet so much better. It was confusing and almost too good to be true."

If you've ever seen the movie *War Dogs*, this was my moment of banging my head against the corridor wall. We probably could have doubled our price and still won the work. But it was also a key learning. Being seen as an international, specialist agency for the pharmaceutical drug development and manufacturing industry carried a premium, so we had to price accordingly. This was not a small generic job for a local company. We were becoming the specialist knee doctor from Chapter 3.

One silver lining for us was the higher value we attached to the £15,000. With the increase in price, we raised our game big time and smashed it out of the park. When you price at a level that feels uncomfortably high (in your mind), you tend to rise to the occasion. High margin and a better outcome for the client. Win-win.

So have clear principles, constraints, and think longer term when it comes to money in your business. And for goodness' sake, price adequately. Create a business that routinely makes money, be careful with your cash, and always save some for a rainy day (at least six months' worth of normal trading). It's a soulful way of easing the anxiety you feel doing what you do, subsequently giving you some inner calm.

CHAPTER

CLIENTS.
WORSHIP THEM.

ood clients are the best. And the reason your business exists. Never forget that. The minute you think your internal stuff is more important than your customers, you have a major problem on your hands. This chapter and the next one are the two essential ingredients for a solid foundation and sustained, incremental growth for your business. Focus on keeping your customers and staff happy, and that's 90 percent of the battle.

Over the last twenty years, I've heard clients called every name under the sun. The same clients that are paying to keep the lights on. Retention, loyalty, and referrals are what's going to drive your business goals, so aim to keep every good client you get.

Although I've made lots of mistakes on my journey (now masqueraded as learnings for you), getting to know clients and building relationships with them is something I'm so glad I've done. When you really understand a client's business, you can make a serious impact. And when you have a strong personal relationship with a client, you can add value well beyond the service you're offering. I constantly urge my team to go for dinner with clients, take them for drinks, get to know them. Hobbies, dreams, fears, family, stresses—the whole lot. These are the people who help companies like ours grow and give us the most powerful business development gifts in the world—additional business and referrals.

Be proactive about building a relationship with every client in your business. You don't have to be the one who answers every email or call, but when they really need your help, be there for them in a heartbeat. I look at some of the client relationships I've built over the last decade. Many of my clients I would classify as friends. Actually, really close friends. Over the years, I believe I've demonstrated through my behaviour and actions that each client can trust me with work and non-work stuff. For example, clients have come to me for career advice if they are thinking of moving on or to get my take on how to deal with a prickly colleague. Just being a good listener and being objective with your thoughts can really cement a relationship.

In truth, when you supply creative and marketing services like we do, you are never indispensable. In fact, most professional services are dispensable, or at least replaceable. The pandemic has proved that for many. Nevertheless, you want to make it so you are the last place the client wants to cut. Both for the value of what your service delivers and also the fact that it'll be heart-wrenching for the client to do so.

In practical terms, start by doing these five things with each and every client.

1. Schedule regular (quarterly) catch-ups with the main decision maker. At the very least, you should do this with your top 20 percent of clients, and the high-growth ones that appeared in Boxes 1 and 2 in your client matrix. Also, it's good practice to conduct some kind of annual customer survey to help keep your firm's finger on the pulse of how your clients are perceiving your work and the partnership as a whole. Qualitative research interviews work well for us.

2. Ask questions and listen. And when I say listen, I mean listen to absorb. Take notes on all the things your client is telling you that causes them pain. Take the time to understand and be genuinely empathetic. Don't let your mind get sidetracked by what more you can sell them or where you're going for lunch.

3. Be helpful. This could be in terms of work or in personal life. If you don't know exactly where to start, just be generous and proactive about your communications. For example, if you come across a software tool that fixes the pain point your client mentioned last quarter, send them a note. Or, more personally, send a recommendation to your favourite

restaurant in the city that your client is travelling to. No matter what you do, the thoughtful, unprovoked generosity will go a long way to maintain client relationships and keep those vastly important referrals coming in.

4. Be responsive. Even to this day, any email from a client gets a reply from me within a few hours, if not immediately. Even if it's a holding email, clients appreciate being acknowledged and told that you're on it. By setting the example myself, my team understands the standards they need to meet in their own client correspondence. Generally, it's a good idea to treat every client like royalty. And if you do mess up at some point (it happens), for goodness' sake, say you're sorry and try to make it right.

5. Be a connector. Introduce clients to people who will help solve their problems and add value. Because it's the right thing to do, not for money.

As your business evolves and you add more clients, getting the balance between existing clients and new ones becomes harder. Especially when you're the face of the business. Several of our original clients are still customers today, which fills me with joy. I've seen lots of companies like ours chase "big ticket" new clients and lose focus on those who have been paying their bills for many years. Always maintain a balance.

To help, always have your client matrix at hand. A visual trigger to remind you of who needs looking after the most and where your attention is better spent. At a more granular level, simply keep a list of all your clients in a spreadsheet with a column of when you (or the most senior contact in your firm) last spoke to them. This can be managed in a CRM system and linked to your calendar with a schedule of reminders. A good technique I've found is pondering: "If we won this client today, what would we do for them?" Almost reset your thinking, introduce some freshness, and recognise that clients' businesses change over time. What you would do today might be different from what you thought was right yesterday.

Back in Chapter 2, I briefly mentioned the pain of losing a big client. I mentioned it because, at some point, if you have not already, you will lose a big client. Whether there's anything you could have done differently or not, it will hurt like hell. Aside from dealing with the financial ramifications, it can lead to some reflective soul searching. How could this have happened? What could we have done better? Why have they done this to us?

Keeping your client matrix updated can be a very useful exercise in indicating where issues may arise. Use it as a diagnostic tool to spot symptoms of change or bigger underlying problems. For example, a great client in Box 1 could move to Box 3 overnight if they've been acquired and there is a change of ownership. You need to spot and adapt to such changes in a proactive manner. They may want to bring in their own people, so be prepared. We revisit ours annually, but we should probably do it more regularly.

In reality, this is risk mitigation rather than an exact science. We've had perfect client partnerships that have a change of staff that leads to the introduction of someone who we would never have signed up to work with. In those situations, you must decide whether you want to continue or not. This happened to us in 2018. We painfully said goodbye to a client we'd nurtured and loved for years because the new lead was a nasty piece of work. Basically, someone who would have raised all of our red flags if they were there at the onset.

We made mistakes and didn't help ourselves, no doubt. But we tried everything to mend the relationship and appease the new client lead, but they had their own agenda and there was a target on our back from the minute they arrived. Despite my personal efforts to repair the relationship and put new processes in place to improve things, it fell on deaf ears. The individual was just not interested.

They were not a pleasant person. Quite malicious and very disrespectful to my team. The straw that broke the camel's back was an outright lie. I had personally spotted an error they had made in an important piece of communication on the client's website (basically they had used the wrong version), and I notified them immediately. Given where the relationship was at, I also took a screenshot, which is never a good sign. Said person panicked and quickly fixed the error (as if it never happened). I then had a reply saying there were no mistakes. Unfortunately for them, there is a digital footprint for everything you do these days. But such underhanded behaviour was not something we wanted to live with.

The whole saga dragged on for several months, and after the "integrity incident," I called the CEO to say the relationship had run its course. They agreed, and I knew we were walking before we were pushed. Interestingly, I reconnected with the now former CEO last year (there was genuine mutual respect between us), and unsurprisingly, the individual involved had turned into a nightmare. Shock. Not.

On the other hand, with one client we were given numerous chances to make things right, and we didn't. It's never as simple as it seems and can be very nuanced. But looking back, we had the wrong people in place. Defensive, entitled, and unwilling to accept responsibility. The client was right, and we didn't step up. I'm still fuming now, even though it was years ago. The silver lining is I can spot these symptoms a mile off these days. If this happens to you, you must learn from it, but dust yourself off. Look forward and move on. Don't burn bridges. Treat the loss of a client like a funeral so your team feels the pain. The true cost of replacing a client is much higher than people dare to think about. That's why it's so important to hold onto every good client you have.

In my first-ever agency job, the boss of my team, Michelle, asked me to travel to London with a client to attend an industry event. I was just twenty-three at the time, and it felt like a huge deal. Travelling down to the nation's capital on the train. I was there with the client from start to finish, learning about their sector, talking through ideas and just getting to know each other over a few beers. When I got back, Michelle asked me how it was. I arrogantly and naively shrugged my shoulders and said it was fine and I didn't really see the point.

She looked at me and said, "The point was you were there. Present with the client. Part of his team and someone he could talk to. That's it." Michelle was right. After that trip, the client viewed me in a completely different light. He often called me just for a chat. He sought my ideas and valued my opinion on increasingly important matters. Unsurprisingly on reflection, he also began to spend a lot more money with the agency I worked for at the time. The power of investing time and simply building a relationship.

It seems so obvious looking back now, but sometimes you just need to be there for your customer. Nothing else. Like a good friend. And that can form the foundation of a great relationship. Michelle shared that and a lot more wisdom with me in the early stages of my career. She sadly died of cancer just a few years later at the age of thirty-two. I am grateful for the learning from her (among many) and am more than happy to pass that on to you. I'm sure she would have loved that.

CHAPTER

8

TEAM.
ADORE THEM ALL.

]ust as your business would be nothing without happy clients, it's impossible to achieve the ambitions you have without a team that wants to help you reach your goals. Building and retaining a team of people who want to go on the journey will always be a fundamental component to the success of your business. Put simply, you need to love your people as much as you love your clients, if not more. Whether you have a team of two, twenty, or fifty, employed or freelance, treat them well. Really well. Truly successful and sustainable service providers that treat their people like crap are an increasing rarity these days. Everyone is battling for talent, and in order to give ourselves the best possible chance of recruiting the top tier of talent, we must constantly be nurturing our employees.

Hopefully, this comes naturally to you. Your passion for your business will be alluring for others and infectious, in a good way. Your team will run through a brick wall for you. I genuinely adore my colleagues. Even though I push them all to their limits, I care about their mindset, health, families, and treat them as equals. I'm well aware of the dangers this brings when things don't go well, but it's a risk I've been willing to take over the years. As a result, we've enjoyed a healthy staff retention rate with a natural level of attrition. I've been burned a few times for being too trusting, but that's fine too.

It's character building. Hold no grudges or regrets. Shit happens and life moves on.

Adding more people to your team is such an interesting paradigm. More people in a service business generally means more resources, capabilities, expertise, and income potential, which is great. Quite simply, you have more stuff to offer and sell to your customers. But more people also bring more problems, no doubt. There are so many interconnected relationships as your team expands, it quickly grows beyond your control. It also propels you into unknown territory as a leader.

When I started adding more people into the mix, my aim was to create a working environment that I'd want to work in. Fun, ambitious, creative, courageous, and progressive. With never-ending premium coffee options. It was never more complicated than that. Beyond job security and meeting payday, it was about my team feeling that they worked for a company that genuinely cared about them as people. I took time to understand what motivated each person (money, travel, perks, management, etc.) and then did what I could to ensure their goals were achievable based on their performance.

My aim was to get the best out of them however I could. I was also always obsessed with adding little touches that made it a fun place to work. I still am now. In fact, during 2020,

I spent days coming up with new ideas of how to keep our team happy and healthy in the midst of the painful pandemic.

As good as I was at the softer personal aspects, I was a lot less so when it came to career development for my team. One of the hardest transitions you will make as your business grows (and you grow with it) is the expectations around professional development from your team. In the early days, you can get away with lots of fun perks and lobbing a bonus in the mix here and there to keep everyone happy. You're all friends, and the excitement of the company's journey is intoxicating. But as you bring in more talent and your existing team evolves, expectations grow simultaneously. Your team starts to look beyond the beverage options to ask how will your business help them achieve their career goals? I was not prepared for this at all and wish I'd been more proactive in this area.

In the early days, I was so focused on survival, making money, and delivering work for clients that it was never a priority. In my simple mind, if the business did well, they would do well. This mentality wouldn't work long term. I let my team down, but at the same time the unknown brought energy and excitement. It was almost a catalyst for the momentum. We were all in it together without really knowing where we were headed other than upwards. Nevertheless, in hindsight, I wish I'd given it a little more focus as it would have benefited the individuals and the business. Ultimately, I hired someone who was much better at delivering this to our team then I was. So, think about this now because it may happen quicker than you think.

As new people enter the building, always set high expectations and don't accept any form of complacency. Continually assess your team. Every single one of them. Are they good enough? Do they care enough? Do they set the right example? It's actually not too dissimilar to the client matrix you created earlier. You could very easily do a version for your team. Who are the high-performing stars that cause you no issues versus the ones adding little value with a constant dose of drama? Again, blueprint your finest people, look for the gaps, and avoid the traits you know cause you stress. Assuming most in your team tick the boxes, invest like hell in them and give them all the opportunity they can handle. During the pandemic, when doing a Zoom induction call with a new starter, I am watching like a hawk to see if they are engaged. Those clearly distracted and unable to focus on a conversation with me for thirty minutes will have their card marked in week one.

Sadly, you will outgrow some people as your business starts to achieve new levels of success. But on the flip side, you get to see the impact of your business on the lives of those people who stay on the journey. Jim Collins spoke to this team dynamic in his book, *Good to Great*. He described team building like a tourist bus where people can hop on and off whenever they'd like. The bus still has its route and destination in mind, but the cast of riders changes each stop. In the same way, your team may look different throughout the years. Your job, as a leader, is to make sure you do everything you can to keep the right people on the bus for the right reasons and get rid of the bad people as early as possible in the journey.

A simpler question you may want to ask yourself is, "How bothered would I be if this person decided to leave?" That will often cut right to the core. And the answer changes over time. Someone who's firmly on the bus one year might be someone you want off the following year. It's harsh but true. Understanding the reality you face right now will give you the perspective and clarity you need to make the right personnel decisions when the time comes.

Just as you will struggle to keep pace at times, so will some of your team. This feeling of outgrowing people is one I really struggled with, especially if they were nice people. The best analogy I have relates to football (or soccer for my friends in the US). It's like we've gone from the lowest division (a local conference team) to the top league (a top Premier League playing against the best teams in the world). A team that goes on such a journey is unlikely to retain all the same players. Some step up and make the grade, and others fall by the wayside.

The particularly challenging aspect is every time one of the old guard leaves, you can lose a little spirit that made your business special in the first place. But people leave and you will have to let others go. You just have to accept it and move on. It's the price you pay for running a successful business. The reality is, this is what puts a lot of ambitious experts off taking the harder path of growth. The people aspect is just too much, and it can be emotionally draining. Some of the most anxious times in my life over the last decade have related to staff problems in the business. Maybe I'm soft, but I'm certainly stronger for it now. And you will be too. Just don't assume this stuff is a walk in the park.

Fortunately, there is a rewarding yin to this gruelling yang. If you're able to create a world-class working and learning environment that gives people the freedom to fly, some will truly soar. Seeing the ones who come along for the ride grow and progress fills your soul with joy. Not only do you watch them improve, excel, and accomplish great things at work, but you also see them achieve parallel life milestones like buying their first car, moving into their own place, buying a house, getting married, or having kids and every milestone in between. Knowing your business and your belief in that person has played a part in their life is truly *amazing*. It's what drives me now. Seeing my team grow, thrive, and succeed like I have at work and in life. Creating the leaders of tomorrow. And giving them a stage to do it is an incredible honour.

In the summer of 2019, I travelled back to the UK from the US to attend the wedding of my second-ever employee at ramarketing. A gorgeous, sunny afternoon in a converted barn in Northumberland that was transformed into a stunning venue. Naturally, I was so proud of Holli and just delighted to see her smiling as she married her college sweetheart. Her mum (who lived elsewhere in the UK) gave me an almighty cuddle when she saw me and said, "Thank you for looking after my daughter." I almost welled up on the spot. It was a precious moment that I will cherish for the rest of my life.

At one point, later in the evening, my wife and I were sitting at a table. We had become those older, more sensible people watching the chaos and hilarity of what was happening on the dance floor. There I could see the best part of twenty of my team dancing, smiling, and just showering

Holli with love and laughter. I can picture the moment like it was yesterday. Captured forever in my memory like a scene from a movie that never leaves you. It was one of the most beautiful moments of my career journey. Whatever way I looked at it, ramarketing had brought these people together and created this delicious moment in time. Done right, your business can change the lives of others in a meaningful manner and achieve more for people than you can ever dream of. Well beyond you and your world. So, give your team everything you can, and life may just pay you back in spades well beyond what happens at work.

CHAPTER

9

HIRE.
BETTER
EVERY TIME.

A s you recalibrate and refine your company's focus, evaluating the talent you have in your business as covered will become the norm. So, unless you intentionally opt to stay a particular size or retain everyone (unlikely), bringing new people on board will become a frequent occurrence, especially if you nail what I've outlined in the book so far.

You certainly can't keep doing everything yourself. I'm going to talk about this transition as it applies to you later, but you're going to need to get used to bringing new people on board. I know firsthand how daunting and risky this can feel. You'll get some wrong, no doubt. In all my years, I've got a third wrong. Hire slow, fire fast is a mantra I love, but have not followed enough myself. Maybe you can do this better.

Nevertheless, I've learnt a great deal along the way that will help you. To keep things simple, I've split this into two areas:

1. Hiring freelancers (or contractors)
2. Hiring employees

HIRING FREELANCERS (OR CONTRACTORS)

In the early days, my approach was trial by freelance. It was actually a sensible and sustainable way of growing without adding too much fixed overhead. I'd identify and interview the candidate and then pretty quickly offer them a project. Key things I wanted to know was their rate, availability, and what they were truly awesome at. I'd ask: "What would a dream project look like that you could knock out of the park better than anyone?" I then cast them for such a project.

I had nothing to lose. If they were as good as they said they were, then I'd see it. Sure, it was a bit more expensive, but the margins were clear and still healthy, without the downtime you get with employees. If you're fearful of hiring people like I was, try freelancers first. It's dipping your toe in the water and maybe have a little paddle.

Freelancers are also an excellent resource for situations where you need to bring in niche market expertise without committing to a full-time employee. Just as you wouldn't with full-time employees, don't hire twenty contractors overnight. Find and trial a load of folks for the competence your business needs. You can spend time after you've seen what each person is capable of and then decide who you want to develop a longer relationship with, and who won't be a good fit for your business. You may find that some of these people transition and graduate from contractor to employee over time.

In your evaluation of different freelancers, look for how they interact with your team. Are they a good egg? Do they demonstrate the care for clients you require? Do they have a sense of humour? Some of the nuanced good stuff I personally look for. It's hard to truly get a feel for this through an interview process, especially with service professionals. In my business, PR people, for example, are naturally very good at impressing and saying the right thing in an interview. I mean, they have literally trained people on how to behave with the media. But in reality, some can talk the talk, but can't walk the walk. The try-before-you-buy freelance approach helps expose what is true and what is, ahem, embellished. Of course, in some of your faster-paced evaluations, you might end up making the wrong call about an individual. Good freelancers may have a bad week and slip through your fingers. But having some core questions and standards in place certainly minimises the risk.

Above all, remember to treat freelancers really well, like a genuine team member and not a supplier if you hope to get the best out of them. For me, this meant inviting them to staff gatherings and paying invoices within a few days. Treat them the opposite of mean, to keep them keen. Even to this day, I have personal friendships with almost every contractor we have ever worked with, even if we don't use them these days. Many are often well-networked, so treating them badly is going to do your reputation serious harm. And you never know when you may need them in the future.

HIRING EMPLOYEES

How do you currently select people? It's one of the most common questions I get. The truth is, even when we have no vacancies, we're always recruiting. At a very simple level, I look at these two things, which is 90 percent of it in my eyes:

1. Do they have the specific capability we need for the role we need to fill? At the most basic level, do they have the precise skills and experience to do the job we need them to do (very important if you have a new refined focus). If you're going to be pitching yourself as the best in the world at market research in the banking industry, then you better have these experts. Always aim to hire people who are better than you are. The best hires I've ever made often produce a task during the recruitment process that blows my mind in the sense I know our existing team could not produce something like that (in a good way).

2. Secondly, will they fit in and be able to enhance our culture? Hiring a world-class technician that is political and narcissistic is not ideal for most

company cultures. But if that's your ethos of choice, go for it. This is one of the reasons I assess every new candidate by our company values (literally a checklist) during the interview. I quite literally tick the box whether I feel they meet the requirements or not. This is super subjective, but you can plant questions in the interview that stress test them and give you an indication. I've tried IQ testing and all the fancy stuff in the past. Nothing replaces your gut and feeling those niggles. Especially in a people business like mine and yours. I often joke (but there's clearly truth in it) that I often make up my mind within two minutes of meeting someone.

Together, these two give me a sense of the shape of some-one in the context of almost like playing a game of Tetris (if you're old enough to remember). I want to know: Do they slot in nicely while also making us better and stronger? Also, will they help provide greater potential for growth and development? If so, they'll do just nicely.

What are your go-to questions in an interview? A gen-eral chat is not good enough. I made this mistake for years. Be intentional during your interviews or you'll risk hiring a person you don't actually know well enough. The wrong shape in a game of Tetris can cause havoc and take a while to resolve. To help you see what I mean, I've included the eight most commonly asked questions in my interviews (beyond background and specific skill) that I hope can help you when you're assessing newbies:

1. You've obviously accomplished a great deal. To what do you attribute that success?
2. What work experiences have you had that prepare you to be successful in this position? Please be specific.
3. We have a culture of striving for being world-class. What are you world-class at?
4. What in the job spec is your absolute sweet spot and what is maybe not your strength?
5. Tell me about a tough client and nightmare project, ideally a failure.
6. If I called your current boss, what would they say about you?
7. Is there anything that you've achieved outside of work, like a hobby that you are proud of, that has taken years of dedication and self-motivation?
8. How do you continually learn? How would you describe your learning style?

I always probe into learning habits as a good way of spotting potential recruits that are truly passionate about their craft. Ask them how they sharpen their axe, in their time. Note the emphasis here. Using *their* own time. Look for continuous development beyond things forced by employers.

"Yes, my current company paid for a management course for me. And I look online from time to time." Red flag right there. This is not someone in love with what they do. And as you know, this is fundamental to any professional service craft. Whether it's marketing, HR, IT, or whatever. Each specialism evolves and changes, all the time.

It's also important to develop a consistent process to the screening and interview phase. Most of the hires we got wrong are because we did not follow the process. Or I just liked the person and gave them a job. Oops. That's not robust enough as you grow. Our current process looks something like this:

1. Initial screening interview (via phone or Zoom) from either the hiring manager or someone senior. Iron out the big points here. If the salary is $30,000 and they want $60,000, stop it here. Don't waste time taking them through the process. It infuriates me when we get to the final stage and fundamental,

contentious elements (salary, location, working hours, or role) are still in the air.

2. Next, a technical interview. Often with the line manager and someone else on their team. The goal is to get into the weeds to see if they can actually do the job. This is also followed by some kind of task to demonstrate knowledge and capability.

3. The final interview (normally carried out by our CEO) is a presentation and a culture check. At this point, we know they have the capabilities, but we want to know if they are made of the stuff that we like at ramarketing.

Every so often, you will come across a really skilled, friendly, bright, humble, and understated person who has an insatiable appetite for looking after clients and self-improvement. You can just spot a fit a mile off. If I feel like my team and clients are going to love this person, then it's often a no-brainer. Snap them up before someone else does. I've missed a few people like this over the years (often because I was too cautious), and they've gone on to do great things. Sometimes there is not an obvious role you need to fill, but these people will be worth a punt. Even to this day, I get excited like a kid on Christmas morning when I get this feeling. It's magical.

As much fun as hiring someone is, firing is less so. Sacking people and making really difficult human decisions does not always come natural to folks like us. You quickly go from just being someone who is really good at your craft to the person in charge of telling someone else that they are not good enough to work for you. And it's awful if you're not wired like that.

I like to think of myself as a good person, but sometimes you have to be the bad guy. "Letting someone go" is never a nice thing to do. I've had sleepless nights thinking about it, and I almost passed out once after delivering the news. But, unfortunately, if you run a growing, ambitious firm, or you're about to pivot, you're going to have to do this. My advice is to be decisive, honest, authentic, and direct. Don't sugar-coat it; get straight to the point. And never make it personal. It's normally the best thing for them as well as the business.

As hard as it is, act with conviction when there is a culture risk. This is where "fire fast" is non-negotiable. A mentor of mine talked about the harm "internal terrorists" can do in your business. Spreading negativity, poison, and politics from within. Irrespective of how good these people might be at their job, get rid of them immediately. Pay them off if you need to. Best money you'll ever spend. Before you decide to pivot and focus solely on growth, have a long, honest look at your team. Do you have any bad apples you've been clinging onto? If any of your team were to leave, how would you feel? If the long-term upsides outweigh the short-term downside, then your choice is obvious. If you want to make the most of the next five years, you need only the right people beside you. Do the hard work now so that you don't have to focus on anything but your future goals.

Hiring is both a beautiful and wretched thing in my experience, especially in the type of businesses we run. You will forever try to keep everyone happy, but life is just not that kind. Sometimes it will feel like people are screwing you over, or they feel you are doing the same to them. It's not always easy to see their perspective when you're so close to things. Such fallouts sting and burn as in your mind you have given them your all. Use it as a motivator and move on. This is just part of the journey you're on. Potholes in the road. Just remember to stick to your values and treat people well, and it'll be beautiful on the whole.

CHAPTER

10

RISE.
ABOVE THE ENVY.

Over the years, I've seen clients, colleagues, and counterparts (like you) get so obsessed with their competitors or what other people are doing that it mimics stalking. I just don't get it. If people opted to invest even half of this time on their clients and team, then their business would be in a much stronger position. With your new hyper-focus on your specific niche areas, it's time to let any obsession with competitors go. In fact, depending on how hard you're pivoting, the competitors you identified in the past may not even be your competition now.

For my business, after years of competing locally with other smaller marketing agencies, we were suddenly in a totally different pond after we changed our focus. Overnight, we were not competing with anyone at a regional level and were instead competing with a handful of specialist companies, nationally and globally. This excited the team and me. The world is a big place, and there is enough business to go around.

Simply aim at becoming one of the top brands in your chosen segments and sweet spot positioning. For example, if you're a consulting firm for cyber security in the mining industry (intentionally niche, I know), then focus on becoming one of the top three players of that space in the buyer's mind. This takes time, of course, but should be your goal. It's a battle to get in the minds of your prospects, and then stay there.

In some super niche micro sectors, you may even be the first to market. That's an exciting place to be as you can create the category. Land grab and establish yourself as the go-to solution for those you serve. Make sure if a client is looking for what you do relative to their sector, you're front of mind.

In most cases, there will be existing companies battling for the same buyers. Sure, I'd take the time to understand what makes you different or better, which may sway a potential client to choose you over them. But it's very easy to get green eyes when you look at your competition. Look, they are doing this and that. It can drive you crazy. So why let it consume and drain you? Don't get obsessed with them and instead, learn from them. If you're going to get all OCD about something, then focus this energy on your clients' needs, pains, and desires.

I'm not one of those folks who hates my competition or wishes any kind of ill on them. At the end of the day, they are just people trying to do the best they can do for their business, team, and family. Life is too short to fill it with resentment and envy. My view is to always be friendly, kind, and positive to any competitor. It makes it really hard to dislike and disrespect you. I've also learned so much from spending time talking with these people, especially those who are several years ahead of me and at a different point of the journey.

There are also those companies that appear to do the same type of work that you do. But when you speak to them and scratch beneath the surface, they actually do something different. Therein lies an opportunity for an alliance or just a referral partner. In the last few months, I've sent several leads to healthcare agencies I know for projects that are not a good fit for us but will be for them. Instead of spending time obsessing about ways they may or may not steal business from you, build relationships with others in your space. The opportunities to help each other grow will far outweigh any downsides.

To this day, I maintain a positive relationship with all the competitors I know about. A few years ago, we won a big global pitch. It was a big moment for our agency. The following day, I had a nice message from both the founder of the incumbent agency and the agency we were head-to-head against in the final two. In my mind, this is proof that you can do business the right way and be respected for it. And that's important to me. This is the right way to behave.

On the flip side, I recall one competitor from the early days who became obsessed with us. This is the type of person who would shun you at an event when you said hello and remove your connection on LinkedIn to avoid being confronted with your success. Mature and classy, right? His business has not moved on in five years. They're focusing on the wrong thing. I also had another one that almost fell off her chair when I said hello at an event and said I admired the company she had built. Decide right now that you'll be kind and open to everyone in your space. It'll be a small change that will provide endless rewards as you grow bigger and bigger. To each their own, but think about where you want to focus your energy and how you want to behave.

Don't for one second think this makes me soft or not competitive. Or that I am asking you to do the same. Far from it. The way I look at this, and I hope you do too, is to channel that competitive spirit into improving yourself, galvanising your team, and really supercharging your business. That takes care of the competition in its own way—the right way.

There is one interesting quirk to all of this competitor chat as your business evolves and establishes itself in a space. The thing that should keep you on your toes is not the competitors you have today but the ones you will have tomorrow. Earth is a very different place post-COVID, and in my mind, it has made the world smaller from a communications and technology perspective. Specific expertise is available online, 24/7. This is why you need to continually work at improving your offering, your team, and your client experience to build trust and loyalty. Do not stand still or get complacent for even a second. Comfort can be fatal.

The final suggestion I have for you is to spend time with noncompetitive company owners just like you. I am part of a group of agency owners in the US and one in the UK. This is all about growing, sharing best practices, new tools, experiences, common pains, and other important conversations to grow as a person and a business leader. Again, it's about learning, improving, and adapting. Most companies that have similar capabilities to you will not be in competition with you, so why would you not learn from them? They all face the same challenges. For example, I recently connected with a niche agency owner in the licensing world. Despite catering to totally different markets, we had lots in common and could learn from one another.

In summary, don't be jealous, even for an instant. And don't measure yourself or your company by looking at others, as it leads to greed and desire. It's a really slippery slope. Instead, share insights and expand your knowledge. And focus on spending your energy and attention obsessing over customers and your team. This will go a long way with dealing with your competition.

CHAPTER

11

TAKE INVESTMENT.
OR NOT.

t was late March 2017. A typically brisk day in Newcastle for that time of year. Or for any time of the year for the North East of England in fact. I remember the day well. I'd arranged to meet a guy who I'd leaned on for advice in the previous year as a mentor. He was someone whom I greatly admired, who had grown an agency to a scale that was unimaginable for me at the time. We sat down in the type of hipster coffee place that you'd expect two agency leaders to meet. Lots of chequered shirts, beards, industrial lights, and expensive tiny lattes. You know the type of place.

I thought it was just a general catch-up. After the standard chitchat, he said,

"So, listen, I'd be interested in buying your agency. We are financing the creation of a bigger agency group, and I'd like your business to be the PR and content arm of the group." He took a pen and piece of paper to illustrate the group and where ramarketing would slot in. They call it an "industry roll-up."

What. The. Fuck. Raman the Rabbit in the headlights. I have no idea how I responded other than I remember feeling a bit queasy. Someone I'd massively respected for many years was interested in *buying* my company. *My* company. Insane. He talked me through the plans and how such a deal would all work. He told me to think about it and speak to his investment guy. Investment guy? For a moment I thought I was in the *Wolf of Wall Street* and wanted to start beating my chest.

A few days later, I spoke to the nice money man. He said, "Based on your numbers, we'd probably be looking at a transaction of around £2.5–3 million." Once again, that queasy feeling. Flattered, confused, excited. Some of the emotions I felt at the time. I'd never set up or grown my business to exit. We were just, well, doing. £2.5 million (about $3.5m) may or may not sound like a huge amount to you, but it was astronomical for me especially at the time. I earned £45,000 at that point. You can see why I had a hot flash.

Flustered, I did what I normally would when something monumental was happening. I called my mentor, Fiona (Fi) and told her I'd been propositioned. As someone who had built and sold her business ten years earlier, I knew she'd get it. Excitedly she said, "Oooh, this is interesting. This, my friend, is validation. You're doing something right."

Let's be clear. The money wasn't sitting on a table in a briefcase in front of me like in a dramatic movie scene. It was simply a stated intention. I had not started my business to exit and make millions. I was never savvy enough to even think like that. My model was simpler—do good work and make money, every month. I get it was a big chunk of change. But a big payday was not the motivator at this point. My team and I were on a journey. Playing the underdog role and ruffling feathers against global agencies. That was just too much fun to walk away from.

If you're ever in this situation, then go back to your list of no future regrets that you came up with at the start of the book. *What must you do in the next decade, otherwise, you'll regret it?*

One of mine was: "fuck it" to doubt and see how far I could take my company.

I was very much on this path by this point. I had a very clear vision of the type of company I was building. As did my team. The Tokyo rooftop bar was my guiding light. So, the decision was relatively simple.

If your business starts to take off and consistently makes real money, there will not be a shortage of suitors that are interested in taking a piece of the pie you have lovingly baked. This situation was the first time that I felt like what I was building was real, valuable, and tangible. It seems crazy that it had never dawned on me in the previous eight years. I do, however, think my naivety and oblivious nature to this type of stuff kept me focused on the things that really mattered: our clients and my team.

Having discussed it with Fi, I respectfully declined the offer but felt a thousand times taller. Which is about six feet tall for me. But it did make me realise that I needed to take things a bit more seriously. We were heading into the unknown, and all I knew was that the unknown was bigger.

It's funny as up to this point, I never ever considered any kind of external investment. This was my baby, and it was never about the money. Buoyed by a sense of confidence and affirmation from this unexpected situation, I suddenly realised I needed more experience around me. A few grey hairs as they say. But not just a non-exec director or just more external mentors who could stay pretty hands-off. I wanted someone to have some real "skin in the game." Investment was a route to obtaining the right type of experience along with some hands-on committed contribution.

There is a misconception that investment is all about money. That's true for many, but it wasn't for me. I never actually needed investment in terms of cash (because we were always profitable), so I never went looking for it. But what I did need was help. And help from the right person at the right time.

As you know already, running a company that relies on your expertise comes with all kinds of headaches and heartaches that match the fun times. There's a famous saying among founders, "It's lonely at the top." You're the one everyone looks to and you don't always have an answer. Let alone the right one. When things started getting a bit more serious for our company, I needed support. The coffee shop proposition was my day of reckoning and realisation.

So, as we continued on our path along a completely new level of growth (and strain), I knew it was time to add experience to my team. We needed the kind of person who'd earned more than a few battle scars and was better for them. Someone who enjoyed the good times and wrestled through the bad ones. But this person also had to know the value and intricacies of the life science sector so we could remain focused solely on our niche. Someone to just guide us into waters we've never been before. And given I'm not a great swimmer, I needed that from someone that I trust too. Not some random investor who was all about "ROI." I needed the same person I always call when I need help in business (and often, life)—Fi.

The big difference from a typical investment was the cash was not the driver. And it doesn't need to be for you. We already had money in the bank. So, after a cup of tea in the sunshine with Fi, we agreed to a deal. She would invest (moneywise) and also help me on a more formal level. I actually poured most of that money straight back into the company. It's been four years since she invested, and Fi has helped me think bigger and make some bold decisions. At the time of writing, we are now five times the size. And Fi's a lot more involved today than she was on day one or than she ever probably imagined, because it's exciting. That's not something you can say about a typical investor. The type that wires you a load of cash after putting you through a painful contractual process and then rocks up once a month to "check the numbers." There is another way. So please don't think investment is all about the money. Timing and what they bring to the table are just as important with our types of businesses.

Investment is not for everyone, so please tread very carefully if that's the route you choose to go down. I'm not a big fan of short-term private equity or venture-capital-type support for businesses like yours, especially in its early years of development. I just don't think you need the money, and you'll grow the wrong way. Growth for growth's sake. Chasing the wrong clients. Ultimately, chasing the money, again. These investors make their money via your exponential and often excruciating growth and then move onto the next. Don't feel like you must "raise capital" because that's what happened in the glorified business success story you've seen. For this one success, there are also countless failures. This overhyped mantra was not for me, and it doesn't need to be for you.

I've seen 90 percent of these fashionable "textbook" companies with a "let's grow quickly and sell in a few years" mindset crash and burn without ever making any profit. When the exit number becomes the primary driver of your success, the everyday business decisions can become compromised. It can squeeze the soul out of your business. A world of pain that leaves people out of a job, clients unhappy, and founders left to rebuild their careers. Don't fail fast. Opt to succeed slower.

I will talk later in the book about building your connections and the value of mentors. Your existing network could be an interesting source of investment from people you already know, like, and trust. Like it was for me.

Please remember, not all investors are created equally, so do your due diligence on them before you sign on the dotted line. When you choose this route, you're not just answerable to yourself anymore. There's always a catch or expected return. Sometimes it's best to walk away from that tempting briefcase full of cash.

CHAPTER

12

GROWING PAINS. NEVER GO AWAY.

'm going to end Part I of the book with some brutal honesty. Sorry, guys and girls. The type of openness you don't see in your typical business book. When you take the path I've outlined for your organisation, not everything is rosy and sugar-coated. My reason for telling you this is certainly not to deter you from this path but to simply better prepare you for what's potentially ahead. You need to think hard about whether this path of no regret has enough of an upside to outweigh the downsides. It requires discipline, persistence, and patience.

As you evolve and grow, some problems you have will alleviate. But other newer, bigger ones appear. You also have to deal with things that you're not trained for, and that is ultimately what stops many expert folks like you taking this path. Or what makes them turn back once they've had a taste of the journey. It's just too hard and it's not worth the pain and effort.

As you already know, running a professional services firm from the ground up comes with all kinds of worry and despair. At times you will wish you were a nine-to-five employee who can just switch off. But you can't. And when you go from the little leagues and start playing with the big boys and girls, a few home truths come to roost. Growing pains apparently. Character building, they say. More like hair thinning in my experience!

You'll have growing pains all the time, and they never go away. You've probably already experienced this if you've been going for more than a few years. On occasions where you've made a key hire or won a big contract, you'd have felt like you've cracked it. The answer to all your prayers has just been delivered. But it tends to be short lived. While one problem is solved, another comes up. I once heard a saying from a Japanese business author called Hiroshi Mikitani that a company breaks every time it triples in size. From one to three people, three to nine, nine to twenty-seven, twenty-seven to eighty-one, and so on. I think there is real truth in that statement, especially for service providers. Once we scaled past twenty-seven, the challenges were very different from when there were nine of us.

What also comes with that is what I call the corporate compromise. As your clients get larger and more sophisticated and your team does too, you have to adapt your business. It's not a messy, fun toddler anymore. Rather, you're a maturing teenager working out the world. As much as it pains you, you can't be everyone's friend, stepping in to solve all the problems and picking and choosing favourites. It just can't work like that if you choose to get bigger. IT, finance, HR—I still detest all of this, but it's a necessary evil. Assuming you don't love all this stuff, your only choice is to hire smart people to manage all the operations and keep you focused on what you're good at. To help with your transition towards greater delegation, I've dedicated Chapter 17 to this topic.

As your business matures, the reality is that putting systems and processes in place are necessary ingredients in the recipe for sustainable success. They will save you thousands of any currency in time and effort by not repeating the same thing again and again. It also enables you to set the tone of "how stuff needs to be done" the right way when you're not there all the time. Scaling that "small family feel" is hard, but not impossible. And of course, you can do what I've suggested and decide to stay a certain size. Whatever you choose, just be intentional.

As you go on this journey, try not to let the little things get the better of you. You can drive yourself absolutely insane by retaining and consuming yourself with every little detail of your business as it transforms. Resource planning. The tone of a reply to a client email. Reading too much into what someone else has posted on Slack. I still struggle with this today. It all contributes to that uneasy, floundering feeling. It can be suffocating.

I'm not trying to be a downer, but if you think things get easier, the bigger you get, then think again. The stakes get higher. It feels riskier and scarier. But it's exhilarating and magnificent at the same time. If you are doubtful or unsure at this point, go back to the start. What is it that you do not want to regret in your life? What is driving you down this path? Don't take your eyes off this intentional, meaningful purpose.

For me, the pain points were well worth the benefits. We artificially create glass ceilings in our mind for our business and ourselves. You can smash through these if you want. I'm actually well beyond what I ever imagined was possible for a lad from the west end of Newcastle. And so all the hard stuff I've had to do along the way was just part of the journey and all part of my ongoing development as a leader and a person. The pain was well worth the gain.

Not everything in life goes perfectly to plan. In fact, most things don't. The journey is never linear and as straightforward as you think it'll be, but this is about giving yourself the best possible chance. Sometimes you have to just accept that things are simply outside of your control. You can do everything right for your business, but external factors have the say. The pandemic was a harsh reality of our vulnerability.

When life delivers you an unexpected blow like this, remain rational and calm. As much as you want to scream, shout, cry, and let the earth swallow you up, just step back and look at the situation. It was not meant to be. Reframe it. That door closing will lead you to another, better door. It's about adjusting your attitude and not letting your emotions run wild.

Follow the twelve lessons I've outlined for your business in Part I of the book and you'll give it a genuine chance of success and that sense of accomplishment that we all strive for in our budding businesses. As you take your business on this journey of betterment, you also need to focus on yourself too. The two go hand in hand. Your business won't get better unless you do. And that leads me very nicely on to Part II of *The Floundering Founder* and the remaining twelve lessons.

PART
TWO

BETTER YOURSELF

remember it like it was yesterday. It was the middle of 2015, and the business was changing. It was becoming bigger, more complicated, and increasingly serious. We had opportunities with two sizable international clients, and I knew I had to make a couple of bigger hires. "Galacticos„ is what I called these desired new recruits (i.e., world-class technical people who would take us to the next level). Added to the work pressure, we had just bought our first home and had our first son. Life was hectic and busy in ways I'd never experienced. For the first time in my life, I was seriously responsible for others (wife, son, team) and not just me.

It didn't feel like I was struggling at the time as I was just in "doing„ mode, but looking back, I really was. I was floundering. Big time. I felt like my business was about to outgrow me or go bust at any moment. Everyone who knows me sees a confident, self-assured, outgoing guy. But this was a dark period of self-doubt. I remember thinking, *I'm full of shit. I'm making this all up. I'm going to get found out. It's all going to go to crap, and I will let my family and team down. It'll leave me embarrassed and ashamed.* Imposter syndrome can be a cancer in your mind if you allow it to grow.

Around that time, I knew I needed to make some fundamental changes in my life. I was listening to a podcast, and the guest being interviewed was a gentleman called Hal Elrod, the author of *The Miracle Morning*. I was intrigued by his story and insights, so I bought his book. The basic premise of the book is to get up as early as possible with excitement for the day ahead. And in that "additional time,,, develop some positive practices like gratefulness, affirmation repetition, reading, exercise, and visualisation. Sometimes in life, a book can catch you at just the right moment. This book did just that and gave me a new, more mature, and purposeful direction.

By the back end of 2015, I had a much clearer vision of where I was heading and what I wanted to achieve. The morning routine the book prescribes has been central to that change and has genuinely changed my life. But it also taught me in real time that reading and learning could help me overcome even the trickiest of challenges. I later came across this quote:

"Early to bed and early to rise, makes a man healthy, wealthy, and wise."

— Benjamin Franklin

I don't think I believe in anything more in life than this quote now.

Don't worry, I'm not going to request you get up as early as I do every day. But I am going to ask you to take a long, hard look at yourself and recognise the sacrifices you need to make. By following these twelve lessons, I promise you'll create a much better version of you. A version of you that will shock you, help you keep pace with your business, and keep that imposter at bay. Ready? Let's do this.

CHAPTER

13

SUCCESS.
COMES WITH SACRIFICE.

The reality is most startups fail and promising entrepreneurs with expertise like you burn out after a few years. Most never make much money or achieve whatever they set out to do. Often, because the journey consumes them.

Let's start by acknowledging that what you're doing already, and what you're about to do, is not normal. You are not the mean average. What you're trying to achieve is abnormal, in the nicest possible way. According to the US Bureau of Labor Statistics (BLS), professional consulting firms have an 80 percent failure rate during the first two years. That is staggering and shocking. If that number is to be believed, then you are firmly in the minority already. According to the BLS, only 25 percent of all new businesses make it to fifteen years or more. And ultimately that's what we are aiming for here. Incremental, sustainable, successful growth over the longer term. No crash, no burn.

Given this context, it's important to take a moment to be grateful for what you've done already. You're in the minority that's on a path to professional success and personal fulfilment. After reading Part I of the book, you'll hopefully be full of excitement and belief, and that's great. But will that be there in three or six months' time? What is going to make you dig deep, work on yourself, get better, and take yourself to new heights?

I want you to go back to the exercise that you did in Chapter 1. What was it that you *must* do in the next decade, otherwise, you'll regret it? Those are your North Stars to guide you.

You're now being intentional about the path you need to be on and focused about what it is you're trying to achieve. But how will you know you're heading in the right direction and making progress? Take a moment and think about what success *really* looks like on this journey to these desired outcomes. Not the end point, but the journey. What are the tangible milestones that will validate you're going in the right direction of travel? Think of these as reward markers.

Vividly visualise these success signposts that you want to achieve for yourself by going down this path. When I say vividly, I mean close your eyes and take your mind there in granular detail. Not just the picture but the sounds, smells, and feeling. In the spirit of everything I'm doing in this book, here is a taste of some of my signposts from several years ago.

If I gave my business my all, I would realise these:

- I wanted to be able to buy and move my family to a farmhouse. More specifically, a barn conversion with classic characteristics like beams, fireplaces, an open-plan kitchen (one my wife and I saw in a movie), stone walls, and farm views. I could literally smell the sweet manure.

- As material and immature as it sounds, I wanted a fast, fun car (with enough seats for the kids). I imagined this car sat on the drive of this house, plus the growl of the engine and the crunching noise it made on the gravel.

- Having visited a few big, cool marketing agencies in Europe and the US, I wanted to create a working environment that my team would love, and that people would think, "Wow! That looks like an awesome place to work." I imagined the floor, the lights, the walls. The laughter and vibe from my team. Infectious and enticing.

- I wanted to run six international marathons before I was forty and learn how to swim (stop laughing). I was in awe of those who could run twenty-six miles and live to tell the tale. I imagined crossing the finish line of a world-renowned marathon. The pain and pleasure, excruciating and exhilarating juxtaposition. I'd experienced it via a half marathon, but I knew a marathon would be a whole other level.

- Maybe write a book about all the things I've learnt one day to help others...stop it, you. I'm blushing. You're the best.

By going through this process, you can unlock what you really want and what the "right direction of travel" signposts look like along the way. The things you will work hard to earn. Write these down and review them every day. Yes, every day. Keep them front of mind as you go about your everyday life. Make sure all your little decisions whether at work or in life are contributing. Decisions are much easier to make when they are aligned with a long-term outcome. They're either contributing or not.

We live in a world of instant gratification and ultra-convenience these days. One click purchase. Answers to anything are a Google search away. Oh, there's my UberEATS delivery.

But what you're trying to accomplish will not happen with a swipe of your smartphone or a scan of your Face ID. So, get into the habit of doing the hard stuff first and earn the good stuff on a daily basis. It's basic positive reinforcement, which I use on myself every day. Complete the essential, important, and contributory stuff first and earn that gorgeous feeling of accomplishment. And maybe a little cheeky beer. It's like I say to my kids, do all your jobs and homework before you even think about playing with your toys.

Let's go back to football for a second. If you want to be world-class in your field and achieve such things, then you're going to need to put in the effort and ensure you're world-class yourself. Working on you and your craft, every day. Or as I like to say, just be better than yesterday.

You can't do the normal average stuff that everyone does if you want an above average life. And if you want an exceptional life, then guess what? That's right, you have to do exceptional things. You're already on the right track with your business, but it also needs to be for you too. The two are intertwined. The reality is, successful people do what unsuccessful people are not willing to do. Committing to the harder, longer path means rejecting many other alternative routes. Saying no when everyone else says yes. Doing rather than talking. Giving it another crack when everyone else is in the pub. Believe me, it's no walk in the park.

And the easiest place to find these people are actually daring founders and hard-working entrepreneurs. Basically you. I'd never classed myself as an entrepreneur until I moved to the US. The title is hugely admired and respected in the US. They celebrate creating something from nothing. Creating dollars from cents. Creating a life from a blank canvas for you and your team. That there is the American Dream. And it's rightly celebrated because it's really fucking hard work and fraught with risk.

Leaders like you work double the amount of time to ironically avoid a life that involves half the amount of time and effort! But your vision, courage, perseverance, and persistence have gotten you to this point. And you aren't going to be turning back. It's the founder's curse. You are always online in your mind. I think more about my company than any of my three kids, my wife, my family, or myself. It's insane. And you'll know exactly what I'm talking about. You're probably thinking about it right now. I knew it.

What comes now is even more sacrifice but with a greater sense of intentionality. The type of sacrifice that means truly investing in yourself at the expense of nice-to-do, time-wasting sinkholes. Making time for new habits and important practices that will ultimately lead you to where you're heading. But saying yes to these things means saying no to non-value-adding choices. Being disciplined in building good habits naturally removes the bad ones. It's an incredibly rewarding paradox.

Nothing in life worth doing is ever that easy. And this is no different. In order to achieve the life you want, you're going to have to make some tough calls. The type of decisions that won't win you any popularity contests. But will you really miss a night out or several lost hours scrolling on Facebook when you achieve your milestone goals? No one regrets not spending enough time on social media or video games. They're all traps with a never-ending supply of stimulus to keep you there.

I recall a few hilarious things on my journey. I was once on a stag doo (a.k.a. a bachelor party) at the airport. While everyone else was having a few beers, I was in the corner with my Mac making sure I hit a client deadline. And the second that article I'd written was sent, the Mac was closed. I was fine with my pals making fun out of me. Lean into it. I'm not saying become a complete geek or a total loser. I'd like to think I'm neither. But opt for a useful blog over a social check-in. Opt for a podcast rather than the same old playlist. Opt to drive and not drink on some occasions. Aim to win the day and not look back on what could have been. Simple, everyday decisions that contribute to your goal rather than burning time on shit that really doesn't matter.

Without having goals it's difficult to score. There are a million books out there about goal setting, but my only advice is aim well beyond your perceived capabilities or what you think is possible. When you do what I outline in the Part II of this book, you will rise well above any artificial ceiling of what you think you can achieve.

Let me illustrate. As I arrived at my mid-thirties, I knew my football days were over (sniff). So, I switched my focus to running, and as you've just read, an aim to complete six marathons (having only done two half marathons in my life). Note, I did not aim to do just one marathon. I was aiming well beyond what I thought was possible. The classic shooting for the moon, and even if I missed, I'd land among the stars.

If you've run a marathon, you'll know the training is a killer. Often four to five runs a week, including a long Sunday morning run to get the miles up. Saying yes to that meant sacrificing an overdue habit of drinking too much and partying on a Saturday night. Now, I've run four marathons (having thought that one would be impossible). Do I miss any of those nights out that I missed? Absolutely not. I look at my marathon medals and memories (all done with one of my best pals, Miv) with a sense of accomplishment and pride. Berlin, Paris, London, and Chicago. Some of the toughest and best days of my life. Not one ounce of regret. The parallel with training your mind is, well, unparalleled.

The next few chapters are packed with the kinds of habits and behaviours you need to build or at least consider for the success of you and your business. They require dedication, discipline, and drive. But I promise that creating these habits will kill the bad ones. You'll also keep pace with your business. And leave nothing left on the pitch.

CHAPTER

14

LEARN.
EVERY
SINGLE DAY.

f there is one thing you take away from Part II of this book and implement in your life, let it be this chapter. Make time to learn, every day. *Every* day. Building this daily habit will enhance your life and your business in so many ways.

Come on, let's be honest. Do you burn time on pointless stuff? One behaviour I see in many these days is just a tendency to waste a huge amount of time on social media, video games, and bingeing for hours on boxsets. And COVID hasn't exactly helped matters. Don't get me wrong, I'm a massive fan of movies, and I love scrolling on social media from time to time to see what my pals back home are up to, but the difference is if this was a diet, it would be like eating burgers and fries every single day. And when you eat burgers and fries every single day, you get fat. You get heart problems. And you die younger. Not an ideal scenario. Shit in, shit out. If you fill your mind with pointless crap, then the outcome follows suit.

However, if you change those habits and use that time to actually read or watch interesting talks or listen to podcasts, it's like feeding your body with nuts, vegetables, fish, and good stuff that is tremendous for your mind, body, and soul. Train your mind like you would train your body. Fill it with optimum fuel to energise yourself, and your brain develops like a muscle. I've been into health and fitness for many years. But it took me twenty years to realise I need to look after my brain like my body. You will be sharper, more knowledgeable, "and you'll be well on your way to achieving your goals." You won't get to where you want to be without putting in the effort when it comes to learning and development.

If I look at the success that I've been fortunate enough to achieve over the last decade, this component has been core. An everyday habit's compound effect is huge over time. It goes back to what we talked about in the previous chapter. Making smart behavioural choices and sacrifices about where to direct your attention on a daily basis. Over time, as you see the value, this behaviour feels good and becomes non-negotiable. It's brain training and it becomes a positive addiction. At home, travelling for business, during your commute, while on vacation. It has no boundaries. Learn wherever you are, every day.

Like me, you probably went through school, into your first few jobs and then eventually onto your burgeoning business adventure. Your time, attention, and focus post "formal education" would be on bettering your career, as well as managing social and family life. Quite simply, once this structured education is gone and we don't have someone telling us we need to learn this and that, many stop. And this is the number one failure I've seen in founders. You're so consumed with the business that you've stopped making the most important investment of them all—investing in you. Sound like you?

Learning, for many, just seems to disappear and maybe becomes an empty, recurring New Year's resolution. Don't try to *find* the time, make time. Knowledge is at your fingertips everywhere these days. Don't pass up this privilege. We are so lucky. But it's the fight for your attention that's the issue, so you have to be very intentional about your learning. Again, it's about choice and routine.

It took me well into my thirties to learn how I best learn. Lean into whatever medium is best for you—try books, podcasts, courses, blogs, e-books, videos, apps, anything that interests you until you find the right combination. You have no excuse. Work out what it is your brain likes. If you can't find anything, you're probably broken. In all seriousness, this is a habit for life you need to start making time for. No one ever knows everything, so your learning needs to be on a constant upward trajectory.

So what does my daily learning habit look like (not including anything I "learn" at work)? It's pretty simple and involves just three things:

- Read a useful book (nonfiction) for ten to fifteen minutes every morning. This means I get through fifteen books a year at the very least.
- Listen to one useful podcast (normally while working out, running, cleaning, cooking, or other chores).
- Read one to two blogs or articles per evening.

That's it. A time investment of barely twenty minutes captive and thirty minutes semi-distracted a day. This is about becoming relentless yet realistic with your learning habit. I toyed with the heavy lift of an MBA, but it's a lot to take on. Instead, I asked a bunch of post-MBA students what the best books they read on their course were. Then I read them as part of my own learning process. I know, I'm such a crafty sausage!

My two go-to's are reading hardback books and listening to podcasts. And as I have a memory of a fish, I make loads of notes in Evernote, a digital note keeper. In fact, everything I've noted down as a learning is written down in digital notes. Going back and reading those provided so much depth and insight that actually helped me refine some of the ideas in this book. I bet you've read an amazing book and been filled with actionable ideas (hopefully like this one)... and then a few days pass and the moment is lost. Make notes in the moment and even make time to review what you have learnt. Don't give your brain the chance to let the learning slip through the net. Your mind is the most powerful tool at your disposal, so use it to its full potential.

Looking back at my own life, I got static in my own learning like many people do, especially when starting and running a growing business. It's intense and unrelenting as you know too well. By committing time to read at least one book a month, I have learnt so much and applied this knowledge to my everyday life. The effort has been worth it, and this is a habit I will stick to for life. If you do nothing else, you will massively benefit from ten pages or ten minutes reading every day. Are you really too busy to commit to this?

There's a reason that every "successful person that has made it" blog starts with the fact that the person has a daily learning routine. Reading is awesome. If I'd said this aloud when I was back at school in North East England in the '80s, there's a good chance I may have got beaten up. But times have changed. Dare I say, learning is now kinda cool.

I have read more books over the last five years than I have done in the previous thirty-four years. It's ridiculous. I can honestly say it has changed my life. Remember that sales chart at the start of the book? This habit was created at that pivot point, and this is no coincidence. Obviously not done by design, but it can be for you. Align your personal growth with your professional aspirations and amazing things can happen.

This is not something you can skip. For me, my learnings are not just about business. I've learnt to be a better husband, parent, friend, and colleague from what I've absorbed. That's why I place so much emphasis on learning and growing. Complacency is the devil. For you and your company. One important difference to understand is working is not the same as intentional learning. Sure, you learn stuff all the time "at work," but it's not the same. You must carve time purely to learn and expand your knowledge.

When you look back at yourself from a few years ago, you should scoff at the person you were. Almost like a first-generation iPhone version of yourself. The old version was fit for a purpose at the time, but not now. Today, you are a much better, smarter version than you were five years ago. And if that's not the case, something's not quite right. Imagine what you could be like in a few years' time.

Beware of getting sucked into the daily grind. Better yourself every day. I guarantee that the bald 2030 version of Raman will scoff at the balding 2020 version of Raman. In the same way I today scoff at the full-haired Raman of 2010. I want the same for you, minus the balding issues.

So go now and work out what your daily learning habit will look like. And then stick to it religiously. I use an app called *Way of Life* that allows you to track behaviours you are trying to build or stop (see image). If you're the type of person who likes winning streaks, this may really help you. Oh, and the fact that you are reading this is a good sign. Keep on this track, my friend.

CHAPTER

15

REFLECT.
AND
RECALIBRATE.

'm going to talk about the value of mentors in the following chapter, but one piece of advice that I was given a few years into my business journey that is important to share with you was, "*Raman, it's time to work on your business, not in your business.*"

I suspect you wear so many hats in your business. Pitching. Client work. Interviewing. Banking. Service development. Resource planning. Sound familiar? But at some point, you need to step back. Take a helicopter view of what's going on and make sure you're headed in the right direction. Both for you and your business.

For me, it's like playing a team sport like football. It's the difference being a player in the game and being the coach in the stands looking at the whole field of play from a totally different angle. Same game, two completely different perspectives.

But rather than do this every few years when you feel lost, I suggest you do monthly check-ins with yourself. Get ahead of that floundering feeling.

Firstly, block out a day each month just for you. I choose the last Friday of every month. It's my thirty-day reflection and recalibration. I call these my "create days." I know you're probably thinking, *There is no possible way you can carve out an entire day.* Well, if you can't, that tells you you're doing too much. By giving yourself time and space to plan, think, and create, you will be able to analyse, come up with ideas, and make important decisions that otherwise in the daily pace of running your business will never have happened.

This day is about reflecting on the previous month and ensuring you're spending your precious time on the right things. It's also about fine-tuning your focus if need be, learning, and ideally spending time with mentors.

Some of the most important things that have happened in my agency (including the client matrix in Chapter 2) happened on my create days. Interestingly enough, after seeing how effective they were for me, we rolled the create day concept out to all of my team members. A day off a month to think, create, learn, and be better. It benefits the person, our clients, and the company. And it's just a nice thing to do. Everyone's a winner.

Away from your business, this is actually more about you. Are you on track with your goals? Are those success markers in sight? Are you aligned with your long-term vision? Are you happy and healthy? Again, scheduling regular time for you can help prevent a buildup of pressure, stress, and mental health issues. It's like releasing the pressure valve every so often. It's preventative.

In a post-COVID world, life is tough and uncertain. If I asked you what makes you happy, could you answer?

Beyond the big stuff—your kids, seeing your family, a good wedding, winning a new client—could you tell me specifics? This is where reflection can be invaluable.

I have experimented on myself over the last few years to work out what truly makes me happy. I literally now have a "what makes me happy" list by category. For context, I've no idea how I came up with this process, but I suspect it's a combination of things I've read and listened to over the last decade (there it is—learning again). I call it my "happiness hack," and it comes from constant, intentional reflection. It enables me to proactively engineer the stuff that makes me happy into my days, weeks, and months. So, this is what I want you to do:

1. JOURNAL EVERY DAY.

Before you flick past the page, hear me out. It's not a "dear diary" moment. I use the *Five-Minute Journal* method, and it takes up five whole minutes in the morning and five whole minutes in the evening, every day. That's it. The basic premise of the *Five-Minute Journal* is in the morning, write things you are grateful for and what will make the day ahead great. And then in the evening, what made today great and what you could have done to make it better. You can even grade every single day, which helps you unlock what a good or bad day looks and feels like for you. I'll come onto this in a moment.

2. REFLECT MONTHLY.

As part of your create day, read every page in your journal from the preceding month to capture insights and spot any repetition or trends. I categorise as follows:

- Highlights are simply a list of the good stuff that happened that month I may otherwise have forgotten. I have a list of highlights from every year since 2016. It's incredible to read back as most of us forget a lot!

- What made me happy? This is self-explanatory, but literally any moments that made me happy. Over time, these are precious.

- Behaviour adjustments are basically things that I need to improve as they keep popping up in my "What would have made today better?" section.

- Am I on track? After looking back at my "no regrets aims" and personal success milestones, I ask myself,

"Am I on track and making progress?" And if not, I need to make a change.

Even after one month, I guarantee you will have a few in each category. But the value of these exercises builds through time. Focus on building the habit. To make the experience even better, when you reflect, go sit under a tree, in the park, or somewhere different. Coffee shops, libraries, art galleries, beaches, and country hotels are just some of the places I've been. Treat yourself to really nice food. Let your mind run free and see the sprinkles of happiness. It can be quite an emotive process. I've welled up on the odd occasion. But then again, I'm a little softy.

3. REPEAT, COLLATE, AND AGGREGATE.

Follow this process every month. Thirty days of journaling and one hour to reflect and make notes. Time commitment over a month is just *six* hours. My mum spends more than that a day on Candy Crush. If you can't carve out six hours a month to work out what truly makes you happy and where you need to improve, then you seriously need to look at the rest of your life. What you're doing over time is building up a bigger picture. A picture of the good and not so good stuff, but less anecdotal and assumed. Having done this for more than five years, less and less "new stuff" now appears. You're not as complex as you think.

4. VOILA! SEE WHAT MAKES YOU HAPPY.

This is where the magic happens. And in the spirit of being totally open, here are a few of mine. They may seem obvious, but they make me so happy. So, I build and effectively schedule them into life. And don't worry, new moments of happiness appear if you're present to see them.

a. Running in new places

b. Sunrise and sunsets, any red sky

c. Looking at clouds

d. A clean, tidy house

e. Coming home after work trips away

f. A perfect Friday evening—my boys, my wife, pizza, beer, and watching a movie

g. Seeing my kids with my mum and dad and family members

h. Making dinner for my family

i. Impromptu breakfast/dates with my wife

j. Watching a film with my boys on the sofa

k. Drinking coffee outside on a Saturday morning

l. Pushing myself to the limit, e.g., running, working

m. A sparkling clean car

n. New clothes that I love wearing

o. Beers with my team

p. Trying a new type of coffee

q. Getting lost in the flow of writing to music (basically this moment)

And the amazing thing about most of them? They are nuanced moments in time. And they cost next to nothing. I'm very fortunate that money is not as big a worry for me anymore. But it's certainly not the thing that makes me happy. Only reflection lets you unlock this good stuff.

Starting a new habit is not the difficult bit. Sustaining it is the hard part. The Way of Life app can really help here too. As Tim Ferriss says, "What doesn't get measured, doesn't get managed." So, use something like this to simply track behaviours you are looking to build or lose, every day. You can do this for as many habits as you want, and again, reflecting over time allows you to see where you are moving to the needle and where you're not.

So make time to step back, reflect, and recalibrate. Even if you've had a bad month or some big issues to resolve, this is your time to reset and recompose yourself. It's done and you can only change the future. Using data and insight to work on you like you would your business. And then build these learnings into your daily life. Again, it takes commitment, but you'll not regret it. I promise.

CHAPTER

16

HELP.
LEAN ON MENTORS.

There is a lot written about mentors and coaching, and the value of having such gurus around you. On the face of it, you may think you know what you're doing and don't need anyone to help you get to where you're going. And that's fine. I admire your strong-mindedness.

In reality though, you're probably an outstanding technician. Really good at whatever your craft is that has got you to this point. And now you're finding yourself viewed as a businessperson and maybe even an entrepreneur. Yikes. In that sense, there is so much you will not know beyond simply being really good at what you do. That's what makes the journey so challenging.

The crossroads you're at right now and the journey you're on is no easy one. It can feel very lonely and at times suffocating. There might be more than one of you that own the business, which is great, especially if you have complementary skills. But there is no substitute for experience and having people around you who have gone down the path you're headed. Not unlike the learnings and insights I'm trying to provide in this book. Again, if you think about the analogy of heading up the more difficult route on a hike, you'd be mad not to ask for advice from folks who have already trodden that path. You should never be afraid to ask others for help.

When I set up my first business, ramarketing, in 2009, it was purely to support a client in my spare time and generate some additional income so that my wife and I could travel more. That was my startup strategy. Nothing complicated. But as the years passed, this part-time side project became, well, a proper business. All of a sudden, I was into the unknown and needing to know about aspects of running a business, well beyond my craft in marketing. Unplanned. Delightfully organic and, at times, petrifying. I never wrote any kind of plan for the business until two years in. At that point, I thought, *Oh, crap, I should write something down.*

As you embark on potentially the greatest era of your company's development, it's invaluable to have people around you who have got the T-shirt, so to speak. Seek those who have enjoyed the ups and battled through the lulls. Use these people to guide you into waters you've never been in before. Simply having an objective perspective from those you respect can transform difficult decisions into strategic steps forward for you and your business.

For me, therein lies the value of having good mentors around you: creating the space to ponder what's potentially ahead of me and hearing the possibilities from someone who has seen around the corner. I regularly ask, what can I do now to better prepare for that inevitable eventuality? Not tomorrow but three, six, twelve, and eighteen months from now. Then being proactive about what is on the horizon by arming yourself with the tools and resources you will need. Avoiding any pitfalls as opposed to dealing with the painful aftermath of one. As I mentioned earlier, this was the prime driver behind bringing on Fiona as a hands-on investor. I often joke that she's the boss because I work better when I have someone I'm accountable to. I will not let them down. And quite frankly, it just helps to have someone you can let it all out with and say all the things that are on your mind. It's basically therapy.

So you're thinking, *Right, Raman, I hear you. I get it. I need mentors. Now what?* Well, I'd advise getting two or three mentors around you. I stumbled into my own mentor mix, and it worked well for me to have different perspectives.

The first mentor was someone who had run and scaled up businesses operationally (the nuts and bolts) as the leader and knew all the crap that comes with that daily grind. If you can get someone from the services sector, great, but I opted not to. I went for someone (Hello, Di!) who would kick me up the backside, advise me, and make me face uncomfortable decisions. A seasoned business leader who had actually "done the doing" as opposed to just lecturing about it from the sidelines. I met with this person every month, so I knew

I had to be accountable for the actions and advice Di gave to me. I suggest you do something similar. This person should make you not want to overlook your monthly commitments. It's okay if you're even a bit scared of them!

The second mentor I sought was someone who knew me inside and out. This person was invested in me as a person as much as they were in the success of my business. For me, this person oozes that entrepreneurial spirit and understands my mindset, including the challenges that come with being a founder. It's incredibly helpful if this person can see right through you and read between the lines. As much as they guide you, they can also put an arm around your shoulder when you need it. Think of this person as a coach for the long term. Conversations with them are more about the long-term direction and the overall journey than the monthly stuff—like a compass. This is who Fi is to me. Prior to her investing in my business, we met up quarterly for longer, more big-picture conversations. Now she is probably sick of the sight and sound of me!

Interestingly enough, both Fi and Di were from the pharmaceutical drug development space that we ultimately ended up solely focusing on, so they understood the complexities, regulatory landscape, and client mindset we were in. This was more by luck than design, but no doubt helped as we spoke the same language, and they understood the field we played. Certainly worth considering if you decided to engage with mentor support.

The final mentor I needed, and suggest you find, is the industry pool. Remember our discussion on competitors? This is where remaining open and kind to the people in your industry helps. Use this group to help you attack the business-specific challenges of your type of organisation. For me, this has looked like lunches, Zoom calls, and beers with people who are either in the same boat as me or where I want to be in terms of running an agency. I want to surround myself with really smart people who are solving similar problems. This strand is less formal and almost opportunistic. You will also find that sharing your own mistakes with others in this group can be cathartic and helpful to others.

If I'm wrestling with a particular challenge or idea, I may ask all three the same question. Interestingly, when I took the decision to focus our business as a specialist, the former two above said yes and someone from my creative network warned me against it. It was very helpful as I almost knew the risks and downsides of the decision prior to taking it.

There's been times on my journey when I literally wanted to scream, cry, and find a quiet place to smack my own head against a wall. Growth brings its downsides as I've mentioned. The bigger the success, the bigger the problems, and the bigger the potential falls. You will have no doubt felt the same, and it won't go away.

A quote I once read from Steven Furtick comes to mind. He said, "The reason we struggle is because we compare our behind-the-scenes with everyone else's highlight reel."

This is why you should also reach out to those you admire and where you think you want to be. Some reply, some don't. But by speaking to those in the position you are aiming to be, you'll get a real-life perspective from someone you admire. Too often when you look at people you admire, you see only the highlight reels—the 1 percent snippet of good stuff, not the 99 percent of blood, sweat, and tears behind the outcome. The public glory, not the private sacrifice. That's why having these people around you is so important. They know what it's really like.

Mentors and people who are where you want to be can give you the behind-the-scenes reality and not the fancy front of house. You'll be able to see if where they are is where you actually want to be. So, start writing a list of potential mentors today. The list may evolve over time, but they will all add value to your journey.

CHAPTER

17

DELEGATE.
LET THINGS GO.

What do you actually do in your job? And where do you add the most value? As you move your business forward and evolve, you will gradually do less of the doing. The journey from expert to entrepreneur. Technician to leader. This is a very hard transition for many of us as it takes you away from your core competencies and what got you here in the first place. Handing over responsibility to others to do a job you have done is uncomfortable, but necessary. But why is delegation so hard for us? Normally, because we think that no one can possibly do a better job than us!

This chapter is about identifying and focusing your attention on the right things. The stuff you are truly world-class at and enjoy doing. Going down this route is essential to growth for you and your business. The truth is you can't reach the goals you've set out for yourself if you continue to do everything yourself. I want you to alleviate some of the worries I had for many years, but at the same time, not dismiss or neglect whatever skill got you here in the first place. To achieve balance, you have to be intentional about your attention.

So firstly, where do you focus your attention? When Fi invested in my business, we sat in our office, and she ran me through a little task. A task based around the question of: "Why the heck are you still doing that?" Now, you're going to do the same five-step exercise.

Write a list of everything you do in your company and the time you spend against each month (this is why timesheets are valuable). I suspect it will unveil you are wearing a thousand hats and your valuable attention is somewhat divided. Here is an image of my actual list in 2017.

days

c Real work	8	↓	x 7 days ⑪ gain
I Allocation	1	x	↓ 4 days
I P/L monitor	½	x	
BD Rais³ market	1	x	
BD Lead BD	8	☺	
I recruitment	½	x	
I people mngnt	½		
I financial mngnt	½	x	
BD contract review	¼	x	
I signoff expenses		x	
I Customer issues	1	x	
c client visits	1	☺	
BD events / BD	⎫		
BD networking	⎬ ☺		
BD public speaking	⎪		
BD writing blogs	⎭		
I strategic thinking (ideas gen⁰)	1	☺	
BD prospecting		x	

expansion

① Manc

②. Boston

- client services
- EPS / HR
- Marketing
- BD support

1. Next, review the list and put a cross through the things you detest doing and that are not in your core

skillset. That's the easy, fun, and weight-lifting-off-your-shoulders bit.

2. Now, comes the hardest one. Circle the one thing that you enjoy doing, you're very good at, and adds huge value to your business. This should be your superpower that you do better than anyone in your business. For me, at the time (this may change), it was business development and relationship building. Whatever yours is right now is where you should be spending 50 percent of your time.

3. If you're like me, there will be a few tasks in the running while completing Step 3. Don't worry, you won't give those up entirely. Now is your chance to pick two of these tasks. Use the same criteria as above, but these two tasks are maybe something you don't love quite as much or add ever so slightly less value. Allocate an additional 40 percent of your time to these two tasks. That means 90 percent of where you need to spend your time is now accounted for. For me, it was adding value to client projects in terms of ideas and creating content to be the face of the business. Essentially, what I do today! This should be

the work that is worth $500 an hour (or whatever is a big figure to you) and not the $10-an-hour work.

4. Whatever is left needs to be delegated, automated, or eliminated. If the former, see if anyone in your team is capable of doing these things. If not, hire or outsource. You don't want to be spending your time on this stuff. I see SO many people in your position burning their time doing the medial, easy, non-value-add crap. This is strangling your potential and holding you back. You are wasting your time, energy, earning, and learning potential. Worse, you're not giving your business the best of you.

So what about the last 10 percent? You should know by now that running your own business is unpredictable. So, keep a chunk of your time every day to handle the unforeseeable and inevitable fires that will need your attention.

As I've reflected on this task over the years, I realised it was really an exercise in subtraction rather than addition. As you grow your business in the initial years, you're basically on a learning curve and taking on more and more. Stuff you are literally learning on the job or making up. But when you get to this point in the journey, it's time to be more mindful about where to apply your finite time and energy. Stop sending invoices, researching IT software, and troubleshooting every tiny issue that arises. Trust in others and get over yourself. Realign your focus on the stuff that really matters and that you're good at. The essentials and non-negotiables. Your monthly reflection days should start by assessing whether your time has been spent on the right things. Again, timesheets can help here. If you don't fill timesheets, use a simple app like Harvest.

You have to hand the responsibility to others to be accountable for the things that you used to be accountable for. Like I've said, accept you can't do everything. Hire people who are better and smarter than you at things that are not in your 90 percent. I see this power struggle with many companies that go through this growth. Founders just can't let the details go, and they want to get involved in every facet of the company. This is incredibly infuriating for the team and also holds the company back. I should know, as I've been this guy. So get out of your team's way.

I recall a situation where we were purchasing mobile phones for our team. I was involved in the details around the provider, the handset options, contract length, price, and which team member would get one. What should have been an efficient decision made in a few days by my colleague ended up taking weeks because I was the bottleneck. There was no need for me to be involved other than signing off on the final package. It burnt my time, disempowered the office manager, and also delayed things for our team.

Don't get me wrong. There are some decisions that need your attention, but many can be handled almost entirely by your team. For example, we are currently assessing investment into a CRM system. Unlike the phone situation above, my team has done the required diligence and provided a clear recommendation. I just need to sign it off and we are good to go. Minimal time invested by me, empowering for my team, and a unified decision made in the best interests of the business.

As hard as it is for you to let go, you need to spend your time on where you add the most value. This is the true enabler of transitioning from the expert who does everything to a founder with greater freedom. A business that works for you and not the other way around. To help you navigate clear roles and responsibilities for you and your team as your business matures, I'd highly recommend the book *Get a Grip* by Gino Wickman and Mike Paton. I read this in 2020, but it would have done me a world of good to read it a few years earlier. Based on the Entrepreneurial Operating System® (EOS), it helps leadership teams learn to develop and commit to a clear vision, establish focus, build discipline, and create a healthier and more cohesive team. As a young, fast-growing business, we struggled for years to tackle this until I found EOS. Unsurprisingly, I discovered this from my industry pool of mentors.

Make no mistake. This is a scary and unsettling adjustment. People see founders and entrepreneurs as these risk-taking mavericks. And there's no doubt many are. But, often, we're just pretty normal people who are just really good at something. We have the same insecurities and worries as everyone else. You're just not allowed to talk about them if you're an "entrepreneur." Well, bollocks to that.

This mindset change is hard. You may just have the fear like I did. I constantly wondered, *What happens if this all goes to shit?* I felt that if I delegated things to others and they didn't do a good job, then me and the company would be ruined. I just kept thinking, *If my business disappeared tomorrow, then what?* And I've seen this happen to some of the closest people in my life, and it's heartbreaking. I am in year twelve of my business, and I still have this fear, although it's lessened over time.

To help overcome this nervousness and anxiety, my fallback was to work really hard at keeping my powder dry. For me, this was creating content, speaking, and coming up with ideas for clients and the business. All very much in my 90 percent of priorities. Things I love doing that also added value to the business.

So whatever skill you're good at, keep getting better and working on your craft. Continually sharpening this axe will give you a sense of reassurance like a safety net. Exploring the details and soul of your skill will probably bring you joy, so never lose that passion and sense of curiosity.

I'll use myself as an example. I am a much better marketing expert now than I was five years ago, despite running a high-growth, international business. I've transitioned from being a content and PR expert into a brand and digital expert in the sector I operate. The shift was the result of intense, intentional, continuous learning alongside actually doing my job—a potent combination. As I covered in Chapter 14, baby steps of progress every day, every week, and every month lead to almighty strides towards where you want to be over time. But it takes dedication and consistency. And that's simply a price too big for some. Not you, of course.

That's why I make time every month for new marketing knowledge and drug development industry insight. As an added bonus, a dedication to learning helps keep the imposter syndrome at bay because you have the internal substance to support the external style. Quite frankly, at this point I know my shit if any of my team or clients ask. That's my commitment to them. If this isn't a commitment you dedicate yourself to, you'll get found out and it will unravel all your good work. It's a risk not worth taking. If you pitch yourself as a security specialist in the oil supply chain, then you better be just that.

As a result, I now have an inner confidence that even if my business all goes belly up tomorrow, I've developed a skillset, valuable sector knowledge, and business expertise that I can fall back on. One that holds value in the market. In short, I'll be OK. But it took a very long time before I felt this way. I still have my moments even today. I think a healthy dose of fear keeps you on your toes and hungry.

Don't exclusively disregard your expertise in exchange for "the business stuff." I'm as in love with my craft today as I was twenty years ago. It's a never-ending journey of learning and adaptation. And I very much advise the same for you. Getting better at what you do will benefit your clients, set the right example for your staff, and will be good for your soul as it will give you peace of mind.

I adore the word *Kaizen*. It's a Japanese term used to describe constant and gradual improvements. And over time, this leads to great things. People who seem to be an overnight success (think Ed Sheeran, Kevin Hart, Harry

Kane) seldom are. In fact, they are often the outcome of years of hard work and dedication to their craft as well as a series of tiny iterations. If you read the backstory of these individuals, they put in the hard yards and effort working on their mastery, getting better and better day by day, as well as building their profile and brands. Despite all the stuff that comes with being a famous superstar, they are all truly dedicated to their craft—whether it be music, comedy, or football, respectively.

So, lean into your strengths and do what you want to do. Ideally, the stuff you enjoy that delivers what your business and team need and value from you. But don't forget to keep sharpening your craft. If you want to be regarded as an expert in your area of specialism and market segment, then make sure you put in the work. By the end of this, you should have greater clarity and focus on where you should be spending your time.

Don't let a day go by where your to-do list doesn't reflect the tasks in your 90 percent expertise. If you create to-do lists that don't reflect these top three categories, ask yourself whether you are the right person to be doing these things. It won't happen overnight, but once the transition starts, you'll get good at working out what to say no to. And when people ask what you do in your job, you'll have a well-articulated answer that is intrinsically linked to the success of your business and your own fear-quelling sense of confidence. Whatever happens, you'll be fine.

CHAPTER

18

DON'T JUDGE.
OR BE A D*CK.

Have you ever been at a networking event where you stood on your own with a drink in your hand, looking a bit like a lost lemon? It's as awkward as hell. Then a kind-hearted person comes towards you to say hello. Instantly, this guy or girl becomes your saviour. Plugging you into the social pipeline. God bless them; you could kiss them right there and then. But why are you not that person?

One of the most valuable things I've ever done on my journey without ever really intentionally thinking about it was to build a real network of real people. Not just thousands of random, empty LinkedIn connections and Twitter followers but real relationships. I've lost count of the number of times in the last decade when people have asked, "Hey, do you know someone who can help me with...?" Ninety percent of the time I do, and if not, I can connect people with someone who will know. As my team jokes, "Ask Raman. He probably went to school with someone who can help you!"

Some bristle at the word *networking*. It's such a shallow, corporate word. To get past your initial reaction or pre-existing thoughts on the concept, let's just call it *meeting people*. Much nicer, right? The point is, to be the kind of entrepreneur you want to be, you must constantly create opportunities and achieve the goals you've set for yourself. You need to forget the idea that building connections is only for the sales guy on your team. No offence to that guy, but people will be much more interested in you, your story, and how your company came to be. Even if you're a super nerdy accountant or tech geek, who cares? Harness your passion and the curiosity magnet attached to you. Also, that sales guy will sell himself to another business (possibly a competitor) at some point. So, don't rely on him for your network. Because it's his network, not yours. Get your head up and endlessly meet people.

Firstly, embrace the chance and fabulousness of serendipity. Post-COVID we will all appreciate and cherish social interaction. Maximise this window of opportunity. Opt to keep your eyes and mind open when you're out and about rather than being glued to your smartphone screen wherever you go. Every conversation you have is a learning opportunity if you approach it with a curious mindset.

I've found that exposing myself to new situations, like saying hello to the lady next to me on the plane, or saying hi to the guy who runs the communal area of our office building, or chatting to my cab driver leads to all kinds of new connections, learnings, and opportunities.

Before I moved to the US, I made several trips to the East Coast to understand the market and simply meet new people. On one such trade mission, I was to attend a popular networking event called Venture Café Thursday Gathering in Cambridge, Massachusetts. It was the back end of an exhausting week, and I really couldn't be bothered. I recall my colleagues understandably deciding to head back to the hotel before dinner. That's when I gave myself a bit of a pep talk, "Come on, Raman, you never get many chances like this. Put your phone away and unlock your reserve energy. Plus, it's free beer." Running on fumes and motivated by the sweet amber, I somehow brought my A-game and met several new folks at the event. Nothing earth shattering but just nice, interesting people and deeper insight on the region.

Fast-forward eighteen months, and I'd moved to Boston, Massachusetts. Once again, in a bid to meet new people, I attended Venture Café on a Thursday evening. Free pint in hand, I got chatting to another British guy. We both sensed a strange familiarity. Sure enough, we'd met in the same venue eighteen months earlier. Intrigued by my move to Boston, Michael and I had a great chat. The conversation evolved when I explained my wife (a medic/physician) was exploring career options in Boston. It turned out that Michael's wife was also a European medic who was now working for a local biotechnology company. He offered to speak to his wife to see if she would chat to my wife, Selena, to provide some advice. Long story short, Michael's wife ended up hiring my wife within three months.

Insane, right? An eventual outcome that would never have happened if I'd succumbed to exhaustion and taken the easy option at that original event. Opportunities come from everywhere and anywhere in life. Most of us pass these hidden gems due to another notification on our phone. And in reality, 99.9 percent of these pointless pings in life can wait. What seems important in the moment rarely is the following day. Stop looking down at your phone and lift your head to appreciate the wonderful world around you.

Next, think about the importance of the impression you want to leave. Depending on the nature of your brand and the personality of your business, you should also be a walking, talking extension of your values. If your company's ethos is about preciseness and smartness, then don't look like a slob with your dinner splattered down your shirt. If you pitch yourself as professional and corporate, think twice before going for the shirtless blazer look. In organisations like ours, brands are often a reflection of their founders. Because we have set the tone from day one for others to follow. For me, a big part of our client experience is what we call being "canny." This is a word from Newcastle, the city I was born in and where our HQ is. It means consistently being nice and friendly to people, despite working in a very technical and conservative sector. I believe that likeability factor (not fake smiling through one's teeth) is a genuine, core differentiator. Above all, we offer a consistent matching of words and behaviours. Never underestimate the importance of making the impression you want to make. Literally walk the talk. Pick a relevant style and consistently stick to it. This helps build and reinforce an image in the mind of others.

I recall the head of commercial development at a big pharmaceutical company who I proactively sought out at various trade events over the space of a few years eventually referring to me as "The smart, skinny British marketing guy that always shows up." She then referred me to her head of marketing, and we secured a project. Spiffing stuff.

Let's be honest. You've probably met or been introduced to someone and thought, *This person is of no value to me. Why am I having this conversation and wasting my time?* It's a harsh but true reality for all of us, especially in our busiest moments. The danger of this assuming attitude is it can often stifle great contacts. One of the biggest lessons I've learnt is never assume and judge people. Many years ago, a client agreed to meet me for a drink after work. This was exciting as it was a chance to build a relationship. When I turned up to the bar, he'd brought a colleague who was from a totally different part of the business—operations. In my naivety, I was thinking, *Oh, for fuck's sake. This could be an obstacle to really building a deeper relationship with this promising client.* Anyway, we actually all had a great time and got on very well. I'd let my judging, beady eyes go and just embraced the situation.

Two interesting things happened. The first thing was this client ended up growing very quickly. The assumed "hanger on" was actually the client's closest confidant. If he said I was a good guy, then that was the gateway to more business. It was seemingly a covert test. I passed. Score.

And the second thing that amazed me was said "spare part" a few months later introduced me to a friend of his who ran a growing company. The strength of that referral got us to the front of the line for a major marketing services contract. We won it. It was a real lesson to me about not judging books by their cover and not dismissing people.

Along with being open to new connections, you also need to be intentional with maintaining them. You should prioritise staying in touch and being thoughtful about the conversations you have with each individual. If this is an area you struggle with, I've come up with a five-step checklist for every new person I meet and want to stay in touch with.

1. Capture any notes about the person (personal and professional) in a digital note keeper like Evernote.

Do this immediately after you meet them to ensure you don't lose any of the nuanced, special details.

2. Connect on LinkedIn with a personalised message. Never ever attempt to sell.

3. Send a "nice to meet you" type email often with a mention of something you've learnt about them or an item you said you'd share like an article, contact, restaurant recommendation, etc. Again, this is where your after-the-moment notes are crucial. After a five-day conference meeting hundreds of people and possibly having a few drinks along the way, it's hard to remember all the tiny, but important details.

4. For some, I will also send a personalised video with links to additional resources and just to reinforce my voice and face (helps them recall who I am). You can use an app like Loom or Vidyard to make this simple and seamless.

5. Schedule any follow-up actions, meetings, and just be thoughtful. Depending on the nature of the contact,

I'll be proactive about a "keep-in-touch" strategy with some and will add it to my calendar.

You can take all of this to the next level and add everyone to a spreadsheet, a fancy CRM system, and/or scheduling follow-ups. Just don't annoy people. Build relationships by being generous and helpful. Assuming they connect on LinkedIn, the nature of the content you typically post and share will begin to layer upon the initial impression you left. So again, make sure it's purposeful, relevant, and consistent in style. Make it more about helping them than about you. This is what builds rapport, respect, and reputation. For many of us who work in B2B with long sales cycles, the value of connections only blossoms after years of nurturing and purposeful positioning.

As the years pass and you go deeper into a niche, your network evolves. The quality and relevance increase over time, especially if you opt to specialise in particular verticals. Opt to hang out and network with people whom you can learn from, who can challenge you, and ultimately make you better. Cull any bitter, negative folks. Life is too short for people like that. Birds of a feather flock together, so be mindful of who's in that flock. Sometimes in business, relationships just naturally grow apart. When they do, try not to burn bridges. This can haunt you down the line, so never leave a client or supplier relationship in this manner.

I'm not a ruthless person by any stretch of the imagination, but I have no time for negativity and poison. As I've grown older, I've removed these people from my life. I wish I'd done it sooner to be honest. So, if there are people in your life, especially your professional network, who do this, let them go.

This idea of being kind and just helping people out is fundamental to building a genuine network full of real relationships. Not just phoney folks for the sake of vanity. I'm fortunate that it's come naturally to me. A characteristic that I've inherited from my mum (who is crazy generous). If it does not come naturally, don't worry. It is a skill you can intentionally grow and get better at.

Being good to people, especially if there's nothing you can seemingly gain from them, is just good for the soul. Just play the long game. It often delivers in spades down the line in some weird and wonderful way. I call it good karma. But even if it doesn't, it's still the right thing to do. What you don't want to be is that guy or girl at a conference or an event who's either trying to sell you something or extract what they need. There are people I know like this, and I am loathed to help them because I know their entire focus is themselves and not me or anyone else. It's the classic taker versus the giver. Walking, talking vampire bats (these are real by the way).

Last year, a client of mine was looking for a consultant to assist with a project. They asked me if there was anyone in my network I'd recommend. At the same time, they told me they were speaking to someone I knew who is that classic "won't do anything for anyone unless they get something in return" personality. A.k.a., a vampire bat. They asked me what I thought of her, and I told them the truth. I wasn't a fan. I suggested someone else to consider who in my mind was a classic giver. She had helped me without any ask to get something back. Long story short, my recommendation got the job. She was so grateful for what it meant for their business, it almost brought me to tears. They had to do the hard yards to secure the business. But again, it just shows you how the way you are with your network can have a lasting impact—good and bad. Don't compromise the long-term success and connections for a short-term win. And please, don't be a d*ck.

CHAPTER

19

LEAN IN.
TO BECOMING
A LEADER.

Would you class yourself as a competent manager? Or maybe a leader? The latter can feel like a very uncomfortable term to adopt as it brings a whole superior complex with it.

I'm not a great manager. Ask anyone who has ever reported into me. I'm too erratic, impatient, and annoying. Despite having brilliant people to manage over the years, genuinely model professionals, I find managing people just so time consuming and frustrating, which is why I'm bad at it. I'm cool with that. It's why I only have one person who reports into me these days. The person who runs the company. It frees me to do what I'm good at: ideas, relationships, and momentum. My 90 percent.

Now, you might be a great manager. And that's great. Going back to your list of superpowers from Chapter 17— unless management of people is on there, then you should aim for doing less of it. As your business evolves and your team expands, you'll find yourself becoming a leader. This is very different to being a manager.

Perhaps you've read loads of books and blogs about leadership. And maybe you don't see yourself as a leader in the same way I never saw myself as a leader. It can sound pretentious, superior, and overly lofty, right? I thought I was just one of the gang. That sound like you?

Here's the difference though. As the founder, you're ulti-mately the one who calls the shots. Hiring, firing, scaling up, scaling down. Your words, behaviours, and decisions impact the lives of those around you more than you know. In that sense, others look up to you. Whether you like it or not, you're a leader in your business. To your team, to clients, and potentially to the industry you operate. You're on stage, all of the time. Whether you lead one person or one hundred, it doesn't matter. You're the one they follow. The one they've bought into. Please cherish this honour and duty.

Having had three children, I actually see great similari-ties in being a leader and a father. If I curse and behave badly, then why should I expect my kids to behave differently? I always laugh when other parents tell me they can't seem to get their kids to detach themselves from their screens... whilst looking down at their phone at the same time. I wonder where they picked up that behaviour? It's the same with your team. If I turn up late to meetings and bring zero enthusiasm, then it gives my colleagues permission to do the same. I once read a great line about being a parent that also applies to business: your kids will seldom do as you say, but they will do as you do. So true. I don't think everyday leadership is that different in this respect.

I wish I'd "got this" years before I did. I can't help but think of the many occasions where I travelled with colleagues for hours on end in taxis, trains, planes, and cars. With some team members, I'd set the right tone by immediately opening my laptop and using the travel time to simply work. I'm getting paid to travel, and I'm away from my family, so I will use this time effectively. It also meant that I could enjoy a guilt-free beer and meal when we arrived at our destination.

Yet there were so many times where I ended up "oversharing" with some of my team. I always regretted it the following day. I should never have gotten dragged into that conversation. I shouldn't have said that about so and so. Maybe I was a soft touch and an easy target for some of my team. Get him in the right mood and he'll divulge what he's thinking. Intentional or not on the part of my colleagues, a strong leader knows when to keep their mouth shut. For many years, I didn't. I had a tendency to open up and sometimes be overly negative. This did not set the right tone and did more damage than good. I'm a transparent leader, but everyone doesn't need to know everything. I still struggle with this today, but I have a heightened awareness now, helping me to just button it at times.

I want you to recognise this now and evolve quicker than I did. With this in mind, here are a few areas to focus on.

Things that I work on every day, but that will hopefully give you a head start in acting like a leader and growing into the role as your business moves forward.

There is no shortage of leadership tips out there, so I've tried to distil what I feel might be the 20 percent that make the 80 percent of the difference to founders with expertise, like you. It also takes into account the environment you're likely to work in, the bright folks you no doubt work with, and the nature of a growing service business. And of course, what's worked for me and the journey you're on.

Most importantly, you have to set the tone. I am intentionally reinforcing the point I have just made above, but now I'm linking it to your company's values. You have to be a walking, talking, real-life example of living your values. If a core element of your ethos is energy, then don't be yawning on client calls. If reliability is fundamental, then guess what, be reliable. Set the example you want to see in others. As your team grows, instilling these behaviours in your first five to ten people and setting them as non-negotiable expectations for your leadership team if you have one is crucial. Even to this day, our core brand values appear on a handwritten sticky note on my monitor. A daily reminder of what we stand for, how I need to behave, and what I expect from every person in my company. Nestled in all of this is an old adage: actions speak louder than words. Talk is cheap.

Next, watch your mouth and always be consistent. The fastest way to lose trust with your team (and your clients) is to say one thing only to do something else. Consistency and repetition are essential ingredients to any successful company. Tell them, show them, tell them, show them...repeat forever. Again, watch your mouth. When people (like your team) take what you say as gospel, you need to choose and use your words carefully. Don't just blurt out the next thing that comes to mind. This is something I have to work on all the time.

Also, be a nice human being. Unless your business is consciously a ruthless, cutthroat, kill-everyone, corporate animal (basically most bankers), then your team will probably want to work with good people. Being a good person is simply good business. Get to know all of your team members, take an interest in their lives, smile at them, be kind, and treat them with respect. I've talked earlier about loving your team, and as you grow, you have to systemise some of that. One thing you can't systemise is you. As the founder, you bring the special, secret sauce. So, keep showing your team that you care and that you are a real person (I've even cried in front of my team). It enables them to see that at the end of the day, we're all just people trying to do the best we can.

Remember to learn to listen. There's a reason we have two ears and one mouth. One of my colleagues (Hiya, Lindsay) told me a few years ago that this is what her grandad used to say to her. I say this to my kids most days. I work on this every day, and it's not easy to master! Listening is not only learning, but it demonstrates respect to others. You don't need to fill the silence. It's the easiest way to prove you are interested in and value their opinion. But it only works if you're really listening and actively present while they're speaking. That means no looking at your phone, checking messages, or looking for a new car online. How does it make you feel when someone is on their phone when you're trying to get your point across? Exactly. Don't be that douche. And remember as a leader, learn to listen first, speak last. And ask good questions. It's amazing what happens when leaders actually stop talking and listen. Problems get solved. People grow in confidence. Shit gets done, without you. So learn to shut your mouth!

Show up when it matters, but calm down. Shit will hit the fan at numerous times during your journey. A client will kick off, a colleague will have a meltdown before handing in their notice, and you'll have a major unforeseen IT issue. These are just inevitable side effects of growing a business. When a crisis happens, it's imperative that you are there on the front line with your team and not hiding like a weasel in your office.

But before you show up, take a breath. Present yourself as the calm leader your entire team needs. They're freaking out in those moments, but they can't make the final call. That's on you, and you need to show them you're confident in the decision you're making. I have been guilty of heated, instant, knee-jerk reactions. The type of thing that actually just throws fuel on the fire rather than helps extinguish it. These days, I tell myself to *respond* and not react. The last thing you want to do is react when your thinking is full of darkness and rage. You need to let it pass so you can think clearly. Think of it like fog when you're driving. It lifts eventually. We've all been there when we've spent two hours writing a heated email designed to really hammer home a point. Don't send it. Write it to get it off your chest but avoid pressing send. Sleep on it and decide in the morning if it's still worth writing. It rarely is. Another learning from a mentor, thanks, Fi.

Finally, stop stealing the show. I've had the privilege of spending time with many brilliant leaders. Often, when they walk into a meeting, their previously vocal colleagues literally become mutes. It's bizarre to observe, and I always feel sorry for the now-subdued team. When you bring talented people into your team, you have to learn to hand over the reins (remember the list from Chapter 17) and just let them get on with it. As I write this paragraph, I'm in my fifth week of six weeks off. *Six* weeks off. Precious time to spend with our new baby boy and elder two. Crazy. I could never have imagined that years ago. But as I watch from afar and keep updated via reports, I am seeing my team shine, take the lead, and grow. It's amazing. That doesn't happen if you're always the one at the centre of everything. Therein lies the values of a team and the entrepreneurial promised land beyond just being an expert in what you do. Dare I say, freedom.

A few years back, we were on a team night out (a piss-up, let's be honest), and I recall a conversation with one of my team members about being a leader. He said, "You know why people follow you? Because if we were at war or in a battle like in *Braveheart*, you'd be right at the front. Shouting, screaming, and running into the enemy with the rest of us."

Good God, I'm William Wallace. Freeeeeeeeeeedom!!! In all seriousness, I don't think my colleague will ever know what that meant to me. It was a penny-dropping moment but also helped me recognise what my team needs to always see in me and all of us as leaders. Just be there when it matters. Despite my numerous flaws, by working on the things

I've outlined above, I've grown into being a pretty decent (far from perfect) leader over the years.

But it starts by looking at yourself as a leader. Your team does already. Set the tone, listen, watch your mouth, and chill your beans. Lean into leadership. It's a tremendous responsibility, so respect and embrace it to the full. Maybe minus the Scottish accent.

CHAPTER

20

GUT FEELING.
FOLLOW, DON'T IGNORE.

About five years into our journey, we took some advice from an accountant about a government tax scheme we were eligible to enrol in due to the small size of our business at the time. There was a revenue threshold that I recalled (and wrote down) from an earlier conversation with our advisor. When I knew we were going to pass it, I informed them. Their advice was the tax authority (HMRC in the UK) would inform us if we did not qualify anymore.

The tax world for small businesses in the UK is like self-policing. The guardrails are outlined, and everyone is expected to stick to them. Something didn't feel right, so I did a little research and found out that actually, we needed to declare and let the HMRC know. I notified my accountant and even sent the link, but again, I was told that was "the old way." I made the error of not pulling at the thread and just simply let it go. Ignoring the "something does not feel right" niggle.

Six months later, we switched accountants. And guess what? That niggle was well placed. We'd been badly advised, so immediately we informed the HMRC. Unsurprisingly, we were left with a significant tax bill. Although it was a lot of money at the time (tens of thousands of pounds) that we legitimately owed, it was a lesson worth taking. Follow your feeling and prod away if it doesn't feel right. Don't put your head in the sand, for goodness' sake. There's only one loser in that scenario.

I'm sure you've been there. When something goes wrong in your business that you knew in your heart of hearts was going to happen. If only you'd followed and acted on your instinct, right?

One of the fascinating traits of founders across the board is your intuition. Put simply, most have a gut feeling they can't ignore. Or your secret "Spidey sense"—it's that feeling you get about something before anyone else. This is one of the strongest skills you will no doubt have, so don't ever ignore it. Based on no statistical analysis at all, I suspect your gut will be right more than 90 percent of the time.

I could tell you many more stories like the one above about the mistakes I've made. Several of which are dotted throughout this book. When I've not followed my own gut instinct, nine times out of ten it's come back to bite me in the backside. These words have hopefully brought a knowing, wry smile to your face. Yep, Raman, I feel you.

As our business has grown, I've made a habit of poking when something does not seem right. Even if it annoys my team or leads to a dead end, who cares. It's your prerogative to protect your business. When something jars, dig a little deeper. Many founders are just a little cranky at times as they are never satisfied with anything. This is a gift, so harness your inner crankiness and critical nature as it drives diligence, compliance, and improvement.

Nevertheless, as our business has grown, we've added more experts and specialists. People who know what they are doing in finance, IT, HR, systems, etc., meaning less of you is required. My only advice here is if your gut doesn't feel right and the logic or data validates what you're feeling, then you're probably on the right track. Again, I made this mistake less than eighteen months ago. Another mistake that cost us thousands of dollars. Money well spent as it's going to hopefully save you a lot now!

As your business evolves and you become less involved in everything (as you've delegated most of the tasks outside your 90 percent), look for symptoms. Little coughs and sniffles that something is not right. Just because you transition away from the day-to-day detail, it doesn't mean you can't still keep your finger on the pulse.

At a literal level, one of the easiest ways is to see signs of sloppiness in an office (if you have one)—untidy desks, dirty dishes, full bins, and the like. It's one of the first signs that people don't care as much or are losing respect. As another example, every few months, I review every transaction that goes out of our business bank account. As painful and dull as this is, I can spot something that's not right a mile off. Any hint that we are being wasteful, then I can ask for a full review of everything. Again, as you know your business inside out, you'll be able to spot subscriptions that you don't use, a suspicious expense amount, or an inflated cost that you really need to look at.

Another takeaway here is to keep an "anxious list" or a "list of symptoms." Basically a bunch of hunch things that make you feel uncomfortable or don't sit right with you. Lean into your curiosity. See if there are other related symptoms. And if there are, it's probably a bigger problem. You don't have to fix everything. This is about asking good, pointed questions.

We've covered hiring in Part I, but in a people business like yours, this is where your gut is invaluable. Assuming you've hired people in your business, then there's a chance you've got some of these wrong, like I have. Following your feeling is so important when it comes to recruitment. I've made some terrible decisions over the years driven by an immediate commercial need rather than my gut. Even if someone is absolutely world-class at the specific skill you need, if you think they're a bit off, not in keeping with your culture, or will destroy your ethos, say thanks, but no thanks. Or even better, use them as a contractor so you can keep them at a distance and trial them.

Linked to your gut feeling is that sense of risk. As a founder, you feel this in your bones. Never did I feel this more than when I took the decision to move my family from the comfort of our dream home in our home city of Newcastle to the unknown of Boston, Massachusetts in the US where I'd only visited a handful of times. This is an unusual move for a founder. The norm is to just employ someone in another territory to do the job. But I could sense the opportunity from a business perspective. At a personal level, I referred to my list that I shared with you at the start of the book. What must I do in the next decade, otherwise, I'll regret it?

- Fuck it, see how far I can take my company.
- Experience more of the world in work and life.

I knew I'd regret this if I didn't do it. Thankfully my wife agreed, and she could see how this would benefit the boys. When professionals get relocated to different countries by their employers, there is normally a clear process, lots of knowledgeable consultants, and expenses are all covered. I didn't have those luxuries. We had to just work it out. I can't even begin to explain what a pain in the ass this process was (while running a growing business and juggling everyday family life), but I'm so glad we did. As I've said, nothing worth doing in life is easy. This was 100 percent the harder, riskier path to take, but as it was completely aligned to the two points above, the excitement, adrenaline, and belief took over.

As your business transitions over time, it's easy to be led by the opinions of others and trust the judgment of your colleagues. Especially when your nose-bleedingly busy and focused on what you need to do. But learn to recognise that feeling. Following your gut is your greatest intangible asset. A founder's superpower. When it comes to clients, people, problems, and opportunities, do not ignore what it's telling you. It might not always be right, but you'd be mad to ignore it. If it doesn't feel right, then it's probably not.

CHAPTER

21

GET LUCKY.
BE THE LEAD DOMINO.

One question I've received with increasing frequency as the years have rolled on and my business has yet to become another stat of business failure is: how much of it has been luck? The reality is one will never know. My go-to response has always been, "So much of it has been luck. I'm very lucky." More than anything, I don't want to seem arrogant or ungrateful.

But as I've matured, become more reflective, and developed quite the collection of wrinkles on my forehead, this self-deprecating opinion of myself has evolved. Even writing this book and helping fabulous people like you has been part of this process. There has been more method to the madness than I realised.

It's easy to forget the early days of your startup. The risk. The hustle. The graft. The long hours. The number of frogs you have to kiss. The opportunistic moments. I once read that a successful business is like a snowball coming down a mountain. It takes time to gather pace, but when the momentum kicks in, and the avalanche begins, you best be ready. I'm desperately trying not to use the cliched phrase that you *make your own luck*. But long-established cliches are so as there is normally truth in them that transcends time.

Now you're probably thinking, *Well, how do I make my own luck?* Start by continuing to show up in the right places, like we discussed in Chapter 18. Showing up once and expecting a miracle is not realistic. The number of companies and founders I've seen go on trade missions (like the ones I did to Boston) and just expect new business overnight dumbfounds me. It's like doing a one-off gig with your guitar in the local pub and expecting to be signed by a record label. Show up, again, and again, and again. Be the lead domino.

Embrace and believe in serendipity as I've mentioned. Just meet people, have chance conversations, and be brave. You have nothing to lose. You can't sit and wait for some divine inspiration. Get to work now. Sometimes you just find yourself in the right place at the right time. A perfect storm for your business and the sector where you're focusing. But it's still on you to be in the right place to take advantage of this opportunity and make things happen.

As your business grows and your role changes, you'll need to start saying no to most things in order to protect your time for the 90 percent that matters. But if I'd done that back in the early days, I might not have hired the right people, forged business opportunities, met new people, and grown my business. That's making your own luck. Throwing your heart and soul into it. Keeping an open mind that opportunities can come from anywhere. Being constantly curious is one of the greatest differentiators between where you are now and what's possible for you in ten years. It's also one of the reasons one of the core aspects of my role today is just to meet people and keep my eyes and ears open.

Nine years into my business journey, I left the UK and moved to the US to establish, grow, and run our North American business. No fancy office. No staff. A limited contact book. Ground zero. It was like I was a startup, albeit with the foundation of a solid business headquartered 3,000 miles away. This was a timely reminder of what it truly takes to build a business from the ground up. I was back in 2009 but in an alien environment where people spoke a funny version of English.

Armed with a decade of experience and more confidence based on the things I've outlined in this book, I still had to hustle. Attend events. Meet random people. Have a super awkward conversation with folks who had no idea what I was saying. Reach out to people. Ask for help. When you think and act like a startup, things can move very quickly. Exhaustingly exhilarating, that's how I describe it.

Within twenty-four months, our company trebled its revenues, and our US business was 60 percent of our global turnover. Believe me, this is not me showing off or being arrogant. I just want to reinforce that all this grit and determination, even on a cold winter's Boston evening, is making your own luck. This is forming your little snowball. And there's lots of snow in Boston.

To help your cause, two things you must bring to the table are energy and enthusiasm. These are two of the most underrated characteristics of any successful person. I never appreciated it. This was my ace in the pack in the early days without ever realising it. I'm lucky because that's naturally who I am. A former boss even nicknamed me Tigger!

However, energy does not necessarily mean bouncing off the walls and being overly outgoing, but just simply having a genuine curiosity, empathy, and interest in other people. Even if you're an introvert, you can have a positive energy. Combined with enthusiasm for what you do, it comes across as passionate, which is infectious, hard to ignore, and memorable. These are dominos for future luck. So, if you're trying to entice someone to join your team or convert a potential customer, this way of being is attractive, convincing, and persuasive. It's much more difficult to say no to a person like this than someone who shows little interest in you or their craft.

This type of enthusiasm and wholehearted scrappiness is one of the things that I've seen that separates the real founders who love what they do from those self-proclaimed entrepreneurs who get a load of funding and then sit in a fancy office on a high floor of an overpriced building. These idiots are the ones who fail from business to business and still manage to get funding. Crazy. So please, be the former. Get your hands dirty. Go first. Be brave. Ooze zest. And give whatever luck is due to you the best possible chance. This is your time, so give it your all.

CHAPTER

22

BEWARE.
THE CURSE OF
COMPLACENCY.

"Success is a lousy teacher. It seduces smart
people into thinking they cannot fail."

— Bill Gates

ou've already had a taste of success. And even if you follow 50 percent of my book, this will grow for you and your business. There's no doubt about it. You have the expertise. You know where to focus, and there is so much still inside you to unlock. It may all seem a little overwhelming, but believe me, you can do it. And when you do, others will follow your lead. It all starts with small steps. If you want to read more, then read. If you want to run more, then run. Convert your good intention into action.

So, as we move closer to the book's conclusion (I know, I'm sad too), I wanted to share a few words of warning. Things to watch out for on your journey. Again, I've learnt much of this in real time, so by hopefully sharing my experiences, you can be more proactive about avoiding or being better prepared for them.

Bigger success brings you bigger and arguably better problems. As you move to the next level, it's much harder. The challenges are stronger. The standard gets higher. Greater planning, organisation, technical skill, and training are required. The expectation and intensity grow. The margin for error is narrower, yet the repercussions for any shortcomings go much deeper. And you have to deal with different, bigger personalities and increasing stakeholders. But like me, I bet you like a challenge. Founders are innately good at solving seemingly difficult problems. The entirety of Part II of this book is designed to better prepare you for what's coming for your business. The last thing you want is for your business to outgrow you. I've seen this, and it's sad when the founder is ushered to one side to focus on "special projects" from a glass office. You may as well lock them up with a straitjacket on.

So please, please, please. Never get complacent. Irrespective of the success you have, never think you've made it, and that you're all that. Life is unpredictable and can take everything from you in a cruel instant. It takes years of blood, sweat, and tears to build a successful business. And it can all come crumbling down in a moment. I use this fear to drive me every day. It's fundamental to who I am and what motivates me. The thought of it all coming crashing down because I'd let myself switch onto autopilot actually makes me sick in the pit of my stomach. That's why it will never happen. The fear drives me to be better and not slip into cruise control. Fight hard to retain that hunger you had in the early days. Yes, be content with what you have and grateful for what you've accomplished but keep moving forward.

At a personal level, the worst thing you can ever do is think you know enough. Never stop learning. Actively absorb, grow, and progress, every single day. Investing in yourself is the most important investment you'll make. Never forget that. As I've mentioned throughout the book, it also sets the tone for others to follow. The minute I take my foot off the gas, others will think it's fine for them to do the same.

As you and your team get a taste of success, look for signs of complacency and comfortableness in you and your team. Yes, celebrate the wins, but don't wallow in them. The minute I have seen this in any of my colleagues over the years, their card is marked. When it happens, it's important they know it's been noted. Take the time to understand if there's an issue with the individual and provide support where possible. It could be something outside of work, so it's important to give them the benefit of the doubt and the opportunity to get back on track.

Some step up, and some will be gone within six months. Do what you can as either way, you have to nip it in the bud because complacency breeds complacency. It also links back to being a leader that never rests on their laurels. When people stagnate, it can spread as the acceptable norm. Then your culture stagnates. Complacency can infect your culture. And it's a hard road back to addressing this once it takes holds.

Even if you nail a niche segment, you can't halt. There is an incredible Ted Talk by a guy called Knut Haanaes. He talks about brands that were at the top of their game one day and old news the next. Think Nokia, Blockbuster Video, and Saab. Brands that kept doing what they were doing well (exploitation) but did not look forward enough (exploration). I'm reluctant to use the word innovation as it's not always about innovating. Exploring is asking questions, being aware of the market and the world around you. And then evolving your business to better adapt. New products, skills, services, markets, and better ways of doing things. It's all part of not sliding down the slippery slope of complacency. The key is to have a balance of both.

Having experienced twelve years of continued, rapid growth, my team sometimes asks me why we continually grow and set ambitious goals. Because when you aim to stand still or even slow down, others will pass you by. Be prudent but always be morphing. Founders grow companies, but complacency is the thing that kills them. There are a million examples of this out there. Work tirelessly at not becoming one of these companies.

As your business builds cash, you'll potentially become less resourceful and hungry. You can become a bit blasé and therefore weak and vulnerable. So, one technique I advise you to use is the following. Ask yourself or your team: "How would we do this if we had no money? Or 25 percent of the money?"

A frugal mindset leads to innovation, creativity, and profit. I'm Indian; I should know. Seemingly large budgets or a mindset of abundance does the opposite. You become bloated, wasteful, and predictable. It's why the best ideas rarely come from the biggest corporations. They normally buy the scrappy companies with the finest ideas. Or in the case of Blockbuster Video, arrogantly pass up the opportunity to buy a budding company called Netflix. You probably know how this story ended.

Those who continually strive to be better than they are rise to the top. You see it in every profession. The person who started and grew the business is rarely a lazy bugger who does nothing. You and your business are always a work in progress. No one is perfect. So, strive for never-ending progression and not perfection—a mantra my colleague, Yasmin, sticks to on a daily basis.

Even if you don't like tennis, study the machine that is Novak Djokovic. Faced with Roger Federer and Rafael Nadal as his counterparts, arguably the greatest players ever. He has consistently bettered himself and has catapulted himself among the greatest of all time. His dedication to nutrition is insane. Famously after winning a major title against

Nadal, in a gruelling six-hour match, his coach brought him some chocolate. Mr. Djokovic had one small square and let it melt in his mouth. That's it. And then his attention moves onto recovery and the next tournament.

As I've mentioned, my company's growth and my personal growth happened alongside my improving ability to run. And there are some incredible parallels between the two. You and your business are literally a marathon, not a sprint. Having now ran several marathons (from none in 2015), I now know how to do it and what it takes. You can't just do it overnight. It's the result of a clear plan, focused discipline, unwavering time dedication, constant sacrifice, small iterations, soreness, marvellous milestone moments, intentional improvement, and incremental growth. If you look at much of what I've talked about in Part II of my book, it's very similar.

So easy does it, you. Be intentional but be sensible. Avoid a complacent mindset at all costs. Enjoy rather than be consumed by the journey of what you're creating—it's bloody marvellous.

CHAPTER

23

FOCUS.
ON YOUR
NON-WORK LIFE.

My book has intentionally focused primarily on the development of your business and you. Hopefully helping you to face any floundering feelings with a greater sense of belief and confidence that you can overcome them and move on. Obviously, there is a big component missing in all of that, which is quite simply the rest of your life. I want you to make sure that you don't ignore, neglect, or forget about other important elements in your life. If you allow it, your business journey can consume you and everything else that really matters in your life.

I've seen many founders and entrepreneurs like you grow their business exponentially, yet massively sacrifice other areas of their lives. Most live to regret it. Broken marriages, family fallouts, substance abuse, alcoholism, and irreparable relationships with their kids. This is not something I want for you. Don't be wealthy and unhealthy.

I get it though. You're soooooo busy. Being busy seems to be like a badge of honour these days. Please beware of this trap. It's very dangerous for you and the rest of your life. Being "too busy" at work will impact your personal development and your personal life. It also sets a terrible example for your team. We've probably all said or felt these things:

I'm too busy to work out today...

I'm too busy to read today...

I'm too busy to play with my kids today...
I'm too busy to attend that webinar today, so I'll skip it.
Your business will suffocate you if you allow it to.

Debbie Millman says that being busy is a matter of choice. And she's so right. Never forget that. Especially in your position where you are the one calling the shots and deciding where to place your attention. You decide to be busy, no one else. You're the one saying yes to whatever is keeping you busy, which means saying no to something else. It's your decision to place your focus in one place over another. Like I said earlier, be intentional about choosing where to place your attention.

Don't get me wrong, I'm not saying don't give it your all at work, every day. But it's about being focused, productive, and making the required impact. It's going back to your list of stuff that really matters. Nail the things that you are untouchable at. It's about outputs and outcomes, not the hours you clock.

The number of times I've heard people just like you say, "I just can't find the time to do it." That's precisely the issue. As I've said throughout the book, if you try to *find* time for something, it just won't happen. This is about *making* time. You *make* time to do the stuff that matters, not find it. Simple but crucial distinction.

So, first and foremost, remember the start of the book. When you imagined the conversation with your ten-year-older self, I suspect what you jotted down covered personal stuff as well as business- and professional-related items. Let those North Stars guide you in terms of setting goals. These are the things you need to make time for.

For me, personally, it meant rarely working weekends. Spending more time speaking with my parents as they get older. Having a date night with my wife every month. Running a marathon every year. Having dinner together as a family every evening I am not travelling. Visiting new places on my travel hit list. All of these take time and intention. But it's time I am willing to make as these things matter to me. What do you need to make time for beyond you and your business?

Sure, there are material items too like we covered in Chapter 13, and that's fine. Don't let these be the things that define you, but they are no doubt part of your journey. Whether it's the house you want to live in, the car you want, or that incredible resort you want to experience. But remember, these are milestone markers and proof points that the right direction of travel is the right one.

One of the best things I ever read was in a book called *Too Soon Old, Too Late Smart: Thirty True Things You Need to Know*

Now by Gordon Livingston. He boiled happiness down to someone to love, a profession you enjoy, and something to look forward to. So, my advice to you is to always have stuff to look forward to. A weekend away, a concert, a sporting event, a new coffee table, some artwork, new clothes. Whatever excites you. The anticipation is huge and half the fun of it. As I write this on a Monday morning, in the midst of COVID-19 in the US, we have a long weekend away planned on Friday. Knowing that is there is exciting and will make me give my all this week. I will very much earn that beer in the hot tub.

By following the steps I've outlined in this book over the past five years myself, I've been able to accomplish most of the things I set out to achieve. Reached milestones (that come and go) and built several healthy routines that are now ingrained for life. And none of this has happened without moments of anguish, awful mistakes, and failure. I mean I can't believe I've got to this far in the book without telling you that I once transferred £100,000 of the company's money to the wrong bank account. Yikes. What followed was a week of despair and soul-searching. The money, thankfully, returned, but I learnt never to do things like that late at night in bed when I am exhausted. Every cloud, right?

As a big advocate for health (physical and mental), please don't disregard this aspect of your life. An unhealthy person digging an early grave for themselves simply becomes less capable of helping those who really matter to them. It's like the safety announcement on a flight—put your mask on before helping others. Don't run out of oxygen while you're helping your kids. If you do that, you're all screwed.

Eat well and stay healthy. It will give you the maximum amount of energy to help yourself, your family, your out-of-work life, and your business. I can't tell you the number of times when I've seen people slip into really bad health habits. Often this is a direct consequence of spending every hour God sends on their business. And once you're on that slippery, downward slope, it's a much harder journey back. Again, be intentional and build good habits that eradicate the bad ones.

When you're outside of work, focus on anything but work. Schedule your non-work life like you do your work life to get the most from that time. Ideally, you'll focus on the things that matter. Whether that's your partner, your children, your parents, siblings, friends, or whoever is important. Be in the moment and focus on whatever it is you're doing. When you do this, time slows down. Things you'd otherwise miss appear as if by magic, and life quite frankly is so much brighter and sharper. The other interesting thing is success in one area of your life seems to lead to success in other areas. Some kind of lucky confidence domino effect. It's truly remarkable.

I have trodden the path I have outlined for you. Both for me and my business. Together, they have enabled me to live a life of no regret. I've seen the world, provided my family the kind of experiences that I could only ever have dreamed of, created an amazing place of work for my team, and obtained all the material stuff I wanted. And, yes, made good money.

But money is not everything. Time is what matters. Experiences with your family, friends, and colleagues. Those cherished memories—that's the good stuff. As they say, you can't take it with you. As we all come to terms with the impact of the pandemic and what came into focus when the world was turned upside down, it's made many of us realise that actually the most important things in life are those nearest and dearest to us. So, enjoy life while you can, as we have no idea what the future holds.

Please make sure that when you sit to plan the next era of your life, aim for better outside of work too. Quite simply— be the best you can be. At the things that matter.

CHAPTER

24

THE END.
YOUR START.

Hello, you.

It's been emotional. No doubt about it. I'm not crying. You are!

Anyway, here we are. Almost the end of the road. But hopefully the start of a new one for you, your business, and your life.

You have done so well to get to this point in your journey. You're genuinely awesome. If you decide the road I've outlined is not for you, that's fine. I'm not offended (wipes tears away). It's not the right path for everyone. But at least you're making the decision consciously and intentionally, rather than letting life play out like most people. You're holding the cards. Make a move and pick your path. Don't fail due to indecisiveness.

If you're finishing my book with a load of notes, ideas, and plans like your brain is going to explode, then I've probably touched a nerve. A good one. What I've outlined is no easy journey, but believe me, it's a worthwhile one. It's time to get serious and disciplined. Focus, focus, focus. That's what will make this all happen. Whatever you do, don't let these learnings slip through the net of intent, without action. Don't delay. Start today.

Maximise your expertise and realise your ambitions. Analyse, focus, and go into it with your eyes open with clear expectations of what success looks like for your business. Love your people and your clients. Aim to rule your niche but don't be a hater. It'll be painful at times. Remember, shit happens. You got this.

For you, leave nothing on the field. Pinpoint what gets you out of bed. Work productively on the things that matter. Make smart sacrifices. Learn every day and take time to reflect. Talk the talk and walk the walk to set the right example. Follow your gut, be kind, and don't be a selfish prick. Get the right support around you. Never think you're all that and iteratively improve, always. Unlock the brilliance inside you. Be better than yesterday. Every single day.

I want you to become the best version of yourself you can, and in turn, do the same for your business. Like a yin-yang, this should enable you to have the balanced life you wish. Don't forget to make time for the stuff that really matters outside of work—health, family, friends, experiences, and memories. A life of no regrets and not shoulda, coulda, woulda.

I truly hope my book enables you to overcome that floundering feeling and helps you on your journey, wherever you're headed. My motives for writing this book were simply to help others who are where I once was. And get filthy rich and famous. Just kidding!

So let's go back to where we started:

"Someone once told me the definition of hell; on
your last day on earth, the person you could have
become will meet the person you became.„
                                        —Anonymous

When your time comes, and these two eventually meet, I
hope they are the same person.

Over to you. Be intentional and go make it happen.

Thank you,
Raman

SAY HELLO ...

ramansehgal.com
www.linkedin.com/in/ramansehgalus/

RESOURCES

BOOKS

Same Side Selling: How Integrity and Collaboration Drive Extraordinary Results for Sellers and Buyers by Ian Altman and Jack Quarles.

Too Soon Old, Too Late Smart: Thirty True Things You Need to Know Now by Gordon Livingston.

Profit First: Transform Your Business from a Cash-Eating Monster to a Money-Making Machine by Mike Michalowicz.

This Is Marketing: You Can't Be Seen Until You Learn to See by Seth Godin.

The Practice: Shipping Creative Work by Seth Godin.

Purple Cow, New Edition: Transform Your Business by Being Remarkable by Seth Godin.

Tools of Titans: The Tactics, Routines, and Habits of Billionaires, Icons, and World-Class Performers by Tim Ferriss.

Small Giants: Companies That Choose to Be Great Instead of Big
by Bo Burlingham.

*Good to Great: Why Some Companies Make the Leap and Others
Don't* by Jim Collins.

*The Miracle Morning: The Not-So-Obvious Secret Guaranteed to
Transform Your Life (Before 8AM)* by Hal Elrod.

Get a Grip by Gino Wickman and Mike Paton.

Anything You Want: 40 Lessons for a New Kind of Entrepreneur by
Derek Sivers.

How to Live, 27 Conflicting Answers and One Weird Conclusion by
Derek Sivers.

The Magic of Thinking Big by David J. Schwartz.

The Checklist Manifesto: How to Get Things Right by Atul
Gawande.

Deep Work: Rules for Focused Success in a Distracted World by
Cal Newport.

*The Slight Edge (Turning Simple Disciplines into Massive Success
and Happiness)* by Jeff Olson.

*Eat That Frog!: 21 Great Ways to Stop Procrastinating and Get
More Done in Less Time* by Brian Tracy.

*The Happiness Advantage: How a Positive Brain Fuels Success in
Work and Life* by Shawn Achor.

*Lost and Founder: A Painfully Honest Field Guide to the Startup
World* by Rand Fishkin.

Steal the Show: From Speeches to Job Interviews to Deal-Closing Pitches, How to Guarantee a Standing Ovation for All the Performances in Your Life by Michael Port.

The Accidental Creative: How to Be Brilliant at a Moment's Notice by Todd Henry.

PODCASTS

The Tim Ferriss Show

Derek Sivers

Lead to Win (Michael Hyatt)

APPS

Way of Life

Evernote

ACKNOWLEDGMENTS

I'm never quite sure who actually reads the acknowledgments section of a book. But it turns out that you do, so thank you! Oh wait, you're looking for your name, aren't you? Wow, this is awkward. Well, if it's in here, that's great. If it's not, just know, we probably have a deeper kind of bond that does not need to be expressed in ink. Plus, I have a wordcount limit.

It's my name on the cover, but writing a book is not a one-man job. There are so many others directly and indirectly involved in the process. So, I wanted to take the time to express my gratitude to those who have helped me on this journey of achieving a life goal over the past year.

First and foremost, my wonderful parents. I will never be able to express in words how much you have given me in life. An incredible childhood, a safe place, education, encouragement, belief, and laughter. All pillars of who I have become as a man, husband, and parent. So, thank you, Mum and Dad.

Next, Selena and my boys, Niko, Enzo, and Ari. Thank you for giving me the time and space during the pandemic to dedicate myself to my writing. All those mornings and holidays where you found me writing at my desk. Thank you for your patience, compromise, and support. Selena, there's no way I could have done this without you. I mean, there is no way I could have done any of the stuff I've achieved in the last twenty years without you, Dr. Sehgal. Thank you for sacrificing many of your own goals to help me achieve mine. I adore you.

Tarun (a.k.a. Tuni), Aman (a.k.a. Omin), Naveen Bhabi (a.k.a. Nora), Nisha Bhabi (a.k.a. Little one), Radz and Minz (a.k.a. Cleopatra), Maya and Jai. Sehgals for life. Thank you for being there for me, keeping my feet on the ground, and expressing your pride in what I do. It means more to me than you'll ever know.

The Walia clan. Mum, Dad, Rick, Aarti, Tony DJ Walia, Shay, Zac, and Lana. You guys rock, and I am so grateful to have had your love and support over the last decade. I don't for one second take it for granted, so thank you.

Fi OBE and grumpy uncle Neil, you know what you mean to me. I am eternally grateful for your belief in me, Fi. Your forward is delicious. Thank you.

Thank you to Sara Davies, George Anders, Gino Wickman,

Tucker Max, and Ian Altman for your time and kind words about my book. So grateful and flattered.

Thanks to my beta avatar sample—you guys helped make this book, well, better. Rob Whittall, Rob Mathieson, Ian Harris, Anne-Marie Bailey, Claire Thompson, Paalan Sood, Rachel McBryde, and Jo Carter.

Thanks to the Scribe family—Emily, Hal, Sarafina, Skyler, Mckenna, Derek, John, Iona, Candace, Samantha, and Caroline.

And beyond the book, there are a few more acknowledgments I'd like to make.

Di—thanks for letting me fly and go do my own thing back in 2011. Your direction and support kept me on the straight and narrow.

My ramarketing family. Thank you for everything. All of you. I don't want to pick out specific people as I'm grateful for each one of you. Yes, you. What a journey we have been on and continue to be on. I told you it was a rocket ship. A special thanks to those who have stuck with me for years through the ups and downs. And the rest of you who have helped take us to the next level over the last few years. You guys rock and never fail to make me smile! Wait, which one are you?

Thanks to all my clients (past and present). You have helped make this all possible. I am lucky to have too many to mention individually, so thanks for your belief and trust.

Sharon, Jan, Lee, Boda, Denise, and Sunil Mehra—thank you for taking a chance on me before anyone else.

As I've said, much of my success comes down to what I have learnt in books and podcasts. So a special thanks to Seth Godin, Tim Ferriss, and Derek Sivers who have mentored me without ever knowing it. Your words have been an inspiration to me and impacted more people than you will ever realise.

I am so lucky to have so many friends, relatives, and connections. Thank you all for your love and support. I don't do it all for the likes, I promise. I am so blessed to have so many well-wishers in life. So, thanks to you all.

A few special thanks...

Love you, Mindy. You too, TJ old fruitcake. And Burke, son, you're making assumptions.

Dan Stanton and Gil Roth—thank you for risking your reputations on me!

Sanj, Aj, and Aman—do your best.

Nursery dads, Glasgow boys, Hardcore, Toon Uni lads, Poker stars, JP crew—thanks for keeping me sane and making me smile during the pandemic and for many years before.

Vik—your inner strength is an inspiration to me and has given me perspective over the last year.

Ade, Manz, Nicky, Mears, Nat GG, Ruby, Rohit, Sunil HPR (especially those Halifax trips!), Shammi, Flynn, Yousaf, Sasa, Solution Samso and Pete, and Steve Ramsey—thanks for believing in me and supporting me for so many years.

And to my wider family (aunties, uncles, cousins)—thank you for your love and support.

Anyone who taught me something, inspired me, and made me laugh. Thank you.

And if I forgot your name, forgive me. I'll give you a cuddle when I next see you.

Finally, thank you to God.

Much love,
Raman x

ABOUT THE AUTHOR

Raman Sehgal is the founder of several niche companies, including ramarketing, a multimillion-dollar international marketing agency that helps companies get noticed in the global life science space.

An entrepreneur from a very young age, Raman embarked on a business journey that ultimately spanned the Atlantic—from a spare room in the Northeast of England to the bustling streets of Boston, Massachusetts, where he lives today with his wife and three sons.

Raman authentically shares his knowledge, mistakes, and learnings around the world as a keynote speaker, podcaster, blogger, Forbes Agency Council member, and guest university lecturer. You can find him online at *ramansehgal.com*.